GAL
EPH
PHILIPPIANS
COLOSSIANS
1 THESSALONIANS
2 THESSALONIANS
1 TIMOTHY
2 TIMOTHY
TITUS
PHILEMON
HEBREWS
JAMES
1 PETER
2 PETER

F

PUBLISHED BY
Fathom Media Group, LLC

© 2020 Kelsey Hency
All rights reserved.

@fathom_mag
Fathommag.com

ISBN 978-1-7355582-0-2

WRITER
Kelsey Hency

EDITOR
Collin Huber

DESIGNER
Erin Brown

All Scripture is taken from the Christian Standard Bible®, Copyright © 2017 by Holman Bible Publishers. Used by permission. Christian Standard Bible® and CSB® are federally registered trademarks of Holman Bible Publishers.

Inquiries
contact@fathommag.com

Table of Contents

"The life giving words of God are inexhaustible & accessible to all."

Why do we study the Bible at all?

If we asked every person with this workbook why they decided to study the Bible, a myriad of motivations and life stories would flood in. But something fundamental lies beneath every individual answer—we read the Bible because it claims to be the very words of God. Yes, there are numerous human authors. And yes, there are important academic debates about the origins of the texts. But the idea that the words between the covers belong to someone other than those who wrote them down is what prompts us to read the books of the Bible. That source is the Spirit of God. The Spirit motivated, guided, and curated— over thousands of years and through generations of authors—a single story of salvation that takes us from the creation of the world to its eternal redemption. We turn the pages of an ancient book to know what God has to tell us. That is a far from trivial reason for reading the Bible.

The living God wrote us a life-giving word. In his gospel, John begins by announcing Jesus is the incarnate Word of God. He is the life-giving Word in human form. Six chapters later, John tells us a story that ends with Jesus asking his disciples if they plan to abandon him. Peter answers, "Lord, to whom will we go? You have the words of eternal life" (John 6:68). Peter expresses just the right sentiment—the human heart longs for the words of life and once we've found them we should cling to them with all we've got.

If you've been reading the scriptures for years or if this is your first time studying the Bible on your own, even if you aren't sure yet that the Bible is what it claims to be, know that God meets your desire to know his words with his desire to give them to you. The life-giving words of the God of life are inexhaustible and accessible to all.

How will we study the Bible?

IN THIS STUDY, OUR GOAL FOR YOU IS THREEFOLD:

① To develop a deeper understanding of 1 and 2 Thessalonians

② To grow in your knowledge of how it helps tell the story of the scriptures

③ To see how the truths of God impact your daily life

To do that we created a system for you to approach the text contextually, critically, and to be changed. Each step in this process relies on the other.

CONTEXTUALLY

Reading in context creates the foundation for understanding. If we opened up a novel to any given chapter, we wouldn't be able to fully understand why it's vital to the plot. Neither could we rightly interpret the meaning of that scene, dialogue, or description. Even if we understood everything rightly, the chapter wouldn't hold the same significance on its own as it does as part of the whole novel. The same goes for the Bible. We miss the meaning and significance of what we are studying if we lack the context. Grounding ourselves in the context of the whole Bible, the specific book, and even the chapter we are studying will create the parameters for interpreting God's Word critically.

CRITICALLY

There's both a negative and a positive way to be critical. Negative criticism rushes to find fault. Positive criticism is skillful analysis meant to reveal what is true. If we come to God's Word looking for the words of life, we can't stop short of revealing what is true. That means knowing God intends to communicate a specific message in his Word—it can't mean whatever we want it to mean. It means asking more questions of hard passages, not less. It means knowing sometimes we will have to work hard to understand a particular passage. It means being willing to learn before assuming we already know. The reward for approaching the Bible critically is often understanding what it meant for the original audience and what it means for us today.

The Bible knows nothing of knowledge for knowledge's sake. There is only knowledge of God, knowledge of God's kingdom, and knowledge of ourselves for the sake of conforming our hearts, souls, minds, and the world to the ways of the kingdom of God. Conforming to his ways is our most natural desire when we see the goodness of all God has done, all that he offers, and all that he promises to do. As we meet the God of life in our study, we anticipate that we will be transformed by the renewing of our mind.

This approach doesn't ignore the fact that some parts of the Bible will present challenges. And it doesn't assume that some aspects will stubbornly remain outside our full understanding. But it does assume that God has given us what we need to find life—not everything we need to satisfy our curiosity. In our study, mystery and revelation will hold hands as we walk the road to life.

"The Bible knows nothing of knowledge for knowledge's sake."

What should you expect from this workbook?

Jumping into studying a book of the Bible can feel overwhelming. Sometimes it's hard to know where to even start. This study aims to remove the "I have no idea what to do" feeling from opening up the Bible. In the first week we will look at the story of scripture and the context of 1 and 2 Thessalonians. After that, we will break down the books into smaller, chronological sections for focused study. The study will follow the same progression for every section.

KNOW IT

In order to study contextually, we have to build our comprehension of the book. It's only when we know what the book actually says that we can start to assess its most accurate meaning. We know we are developing comprehension when we begin to recall specific details, trace the author's logic, visualize the book's storyline, pick up on patterns, and bring its overall context into each section as we read. Without comprehension we risk missing the meaning of God's Word. Comprehension isn't magically conjured up in our minds. Instead it is cultivated over time and starts with repetitive, purposeful reading. We have to get familiar with the words on the page.

Every new section of this study begins with reading the entire book— 1 Thessalonians is only five chapters and less than 100 verses and 2 Thessalonians is even shorter. You got this. After you read the whole book, focus on the specific text for this section. There are four ways to actively read the text we are focusing on:

- Silently to yourself
- Out loud
- Writing out the verses
- Listening to the text as it is read to you (You could ask someone to read to you, but audio Bibles abound.)

For this study, choose a minimum of two of the four methods listed. Your reading works to develop comprehension. When you read slowly, read with purpose, and read for detail.

- The entire book
- The specific passage

You'll find a log in the back of your book to keep track of the number of times and ways you have read large sections or the entire book(s) of 1 and 2 Thessalonians.

On your last read through the section, write down what you observed about the text during your reading and rereading.

OBSERVE

This isn't the place to interpret; it's the place to recognize the details in the words. In the space provided to write down your observations, making a goal to list at least twenty. As you go, make sure to observe where you see the main themes addressed in the section you're studying.

Here are some items to look out for that can help build your comprehension:

· Repeated words or ideas	· Quotes from another book of the Bible
· Pronouns — who is he, she, we, that, this, and it in view?	· Lists
	· Setting and changes in setting
· Connecting words like "therefore" or "but"	· Specific commands, promises, or principles
· The relationship between words or phrases—look for adjectives, adverbs, and the ways words and phrases work together	· Comparisons and contrasts
	· Questions asked and any answers given
· Characteristics of God	· Verses related to the main themes of the book

Before you move on to the specific questions, write down your own questions from the reading. Paying attention to details and listing your observations can jump-start your intellect. Lean into that and indulge your curiosity. What questions do you have? What parts don't seem to make sense? What would you like to know more about? There will be a place for you to write down all of those thoughts.

STUDY IT

After you have developed a baseline comprehension, it's time to focus on one particular section of the book. This study will guide you through specific questions to build your understanding of what the author says with more detail and to decipher what the author intended to tell us. You will work through the text verse by verse and section by section. The final question will summarize the section and analyze how it relates to the Bible's story.

APPLY IT

By the grace of God, the Holy Spirit will have begun to transform your mind as you have studied the Word of God. With a greater understanding of what is true, it's time to ask how this text transforms your thinking about God, your thinking about yourself, and the way you think and act in the world. The applications in this study are intended to promote ways to better conform to your citizenship in the kingdom of heaven.

The application section will ask you to consider three different spheres of life. Personal application focuses on you individually. Communal application focuses on your closest relationships with your family, friends, and church community. Universal application focuses on your involvement in the world around and beyond you.

We will provide a few specific questions to think about in each category, but the space is open for any reflection and application

EXTRAS—THEOLOGY PRIMERS AND STUDY SKILLS

Purposeful study of the scriptures makes you a better student of any book of the Bible. You'll find two tools placed throughout the study to help you grow as a Bible student: Theology Primers and Study Skills.

A Theology Primer explains the basics of a complex theological concept that develops throughout the Bible. The explanation lays out a simple introduction to the idea in order to help you understand it within the context of your study.

A Study Skill describes an approach to skillfully analyzing the text. It's meant to expand your ability to develop Bible literacy in any book and at times, to give you another tool for approaching the hard to decipher texts in the scriptures. Every time a Study Skill is introduced you will immediately have the opportunity to implement that skill.

How is this study structured?

For those who want to work through this study as a weekday discipline, each part of the study has five sections that can be completed each day of the week. In addition to the single "Know It" and "Apply It" sections, the "Study It" section is broken into three smaller parts indicated by the insertion of a quote between questions. The suggested daily approach is:

Day 1: Know It

Day 2: Study It

Day 3: Study It

Day 4: Study It

Day 5: Apply It

How can you get the most out of this study?

Completing a study of God's Word as an individual will likely grow your understanding of the scriptures, the Bible story, and begin to transform your life. But God, rich in generosity, has given us other resources for increasing our understanding of his Word—community and teaching. The intended progression for this study starts with completing the workbook section on your own, then gathering with a small group to discuss your questions and what you've learned, and lastly listening to teaching that corresponds with this section of 1 or 2 Thessalonians.

May the God of life bless you richly as you study his Word. May he enlighten your mind, open the eyes of your heart, and conform you along with your community and the world to the ways of his glorious kingdom from now until Jesus Christ returns.

BELONGING

TO THE DAY

Introduction

Most of us know a Bible story when we hear one. David and Goliath? That's a story in the Bible. The Good Samaritan? That's a story in the Bible. Some of us can even reference them by book, chapter, and verse. While individual stories resonate in our minds, we are far less familiar with the story of the Bible. We will build the foundation of our study by reminding ourselves of the grand narrative of scripture and the place 1 and 2 Thessalonians hold in it. Having looked at all of history, we can zoom in to see these letters in their time and place. The context of the Bible and our books leaves us better prepared to rightly understand the message of 1 and 2 Thessalonians.

GET FAMILIAR WITH THE WORDS ON THE PAGE.

CONTEXT & 1 THESSALONIANS 1:1

THE STORY OF SCRIPTURE

Comprehension of the story of scripture eludes us because we have developed the habit of pulling the Bible apart without being shown how or why to put it all back together. Looking closely at individual elements of scripture carries immense importance. Knowing the details brings nuance and life to our understanding of who God is and how he works. But only engaging the Bible in pieces dims our perspective of the world, what God is doing in it, and our place in his work.

Five incomplete perspectives on the Bible take root when we approach it strictly as a collection of standalone sections: the Bible as principles for living, the Bible as evidence to support the view we already hold, the Bible as a list of dos and don'ts, the Bible as an academic puzzle, and the Bible as a source of inspirational quotes. Each perspective turns the Bible into something it's not built to be.

- The Bible as principles for living ——————— Self-Help Book
- The Bible as evidence to support our views ——— Weapon
- The Bible as a list of dos and don'ts ————— Divine Data
- The Bible as an academic puzzle ————— Textbook
- The Bible as inspirational quotes ————— Influencer

This isn't a full condemnation. God designed the scriptures to affect our minds, hearts, and actions, but the Bible can't be reduced to its parts and retain its power. And as part of God's design, the Bible tells us what it is, which we can determine by **looking at the very first words of the Bible and some of the very last words of the Bible.**

"IN THE BEGINNING"
GENESIS 1:1

"AND THEY WILL REIGN FOREVER AND EVER"
REVELATION 22:5

The bookends of the Bible make it clear that it intends to tell us a single story. When we read all of **Genesis 1–2** we see God created a flawless world with humanity as its crown jewel. God gives both the man and woman the divinely instituted role of ruling and reigning under God's authority as his representatives. Jump to the end of the Bible and we find a world without flaw where humans live, rule, and reign together under God's authority and in his presence. But it's impossible to look at the world around us and believe it's perfect. Both individuals and nations fight for power instead of sharing it. Suffering and pain abound. The natural world inspires worry as often as wonder. If everything began perfect, then what happened to the world? And if the end of the story promises a world without pain, suffering, disaster, or war, how do we get there? That's the story of scripture. The Bible is the story of how God redeems the evil-wrecked world.

WE WILL LOOK AT THE STORY THROUGH SIX MOVEMENTS:

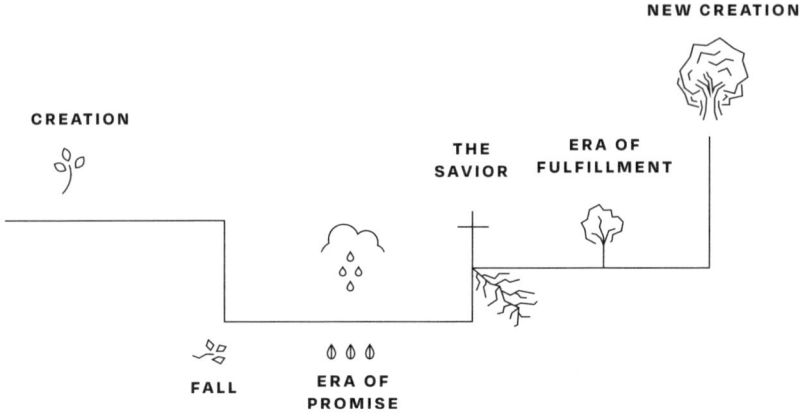

NEW CREATION

CREATION

THE ERA OF
SAVIOR FULFILLMENT

FALL ERA OF
PROMISE

CREATION | GENESIS 1-2

God creates an utterly perfect world to share with humanity as they cultivate all that God's kingdom has to offer.

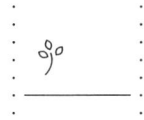

FALL | GENESIS 3-11

Humanity rejects God as king over the world he created in order to rule and reign on their own terms. Having rebelled against all that is good, the human heart is now marked by evil and ultimately destroys instead of cultivates the perfect kingdom of God.

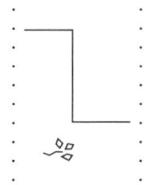

ERA OF PROMISE | GENESIS 3—MALACHI

Loving his creation too much to abandon it to its own destruction, God set in motion his plan to save humanity and all of creation from the consequences of their rebellion and restore his perfect creation.

He promises to do this through one family and the nation they become. As this family and nation continuously give into evil despite their special role in God's plan, he continuously builds on his promise to bring salvation, bless his people, and redeem all things. The prophets make it clear that the human heart harbors a spirit of rebellion. It can't partner with God to accomplish his plan without being remade. But God promises new hearts and that he will establish his perfect kingdom once again through one man—a king—who will come from this chosen family and nation. This king will do what humanity can not.

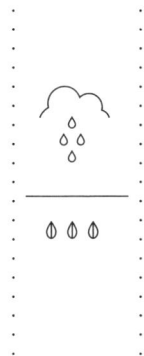

THE SAVIOR | MATTHEW—JOHN

After centuries of God's people failing to obey God and proving incapable of partnering with him to renew his kingdom, God sends the promised savior. A child is born in the most unlikely of circumstances. He is fully human with claim to the throne of his people but also fully God. His name is Jesus and he goes on to completely reject evil and cultivate the kingdom of God in the evil-wrecked world. Jesus succeeds in every way that humanity fails.

His work extended beyond his life to his death. Killed by those he came to save, Jesus takes consequences of evil on behalf of humanity who rejected God. Having instituted God's kingdom in his life and absorbed the wrath of God toward those who reject him in his death, three days later Jesus is raised from the dead, conquering evil and death.

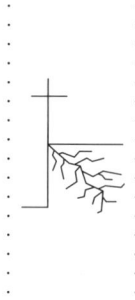

ERA OF FULFILLMENT | ACTS—JUDE

Ascending to heaven, Jesus doesn't yet fully institute God's kingdom. Instead he offers every person the benefits of his life, death, and resurrection: salvation from the eternal consequences of their sin, restoration once again to the kingdom of God, and a renewed heart remade by the Spirit of God.

As he goes, Jesus commissions those who accept his offer of salvation to partner with him to renew humanity. God's people are now able to both share God's invitation into his kingdom and institute the ways of God's kingdom in the world. His people cultivate the kingdom of God by the power of the Spirit of God as they await the day he sends Jesus back to earth, fulfilling all of his promises.

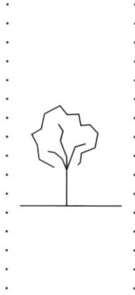

NEW CREATION | REVELATION

At the time God has chosen, Jesus Christ will return once and for all. Upon his final return, the savior will vanquish his enemies with only the words of his mouth to ensure the restoration of all that was lost when humanity rejected God. When God institutes new creation evil vanishes, suffering ceases, creation flourishes, and God's people rule and reign with him as they cultivate the kingdom God he created to share with them.

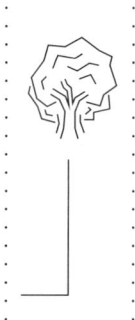

This storyline directs the whole of the scriptures. Every book of the Bible we open, every verse we read is part of the epic narrative that God himself scripted, leading us from the beginning of the story to the end. When we know the story, we can see more vividly the greatness of our God, better understand the purposes of the texts we study, and reveal how the story of each of our lives is caught up in the greatest story of all time.

PLACING 1 AND 2 THESSALONIANS IN THE STORY

1 and 2 Thessalonians were written during the Era of Fulfillment. More specifically, they were written after Jesus's crucifixion, resurrection, and ascension to heaven—but prior to his final return.

That means they were written during a time in history shared with us today. Jesus's offer of salvation remains available to all and those who have accepted it share in his commission to spread the news of salvation and establish the ways of God's kingdom. All who follow Jesus look for the day when he will finally return and install the new creation that restores the perfection and glory God always intended.

THE CONTEXT OF THE BOOKS

Write out **1 Thessalonians 1:1** and **2 Thessalonians 1:1**

Who wrote 1 and 2 Thessalonians?
Paul with Silas and Timothy | Three people are listed as authors of these books, but Paul—as an apostle—is understood to be the lead writer and the primary voice of authority. In 1 and 2 Thessalonians Paul retains the plural "we" when referring to the perspective of the authors. Paul's voice is primary from beginning to end in both books, but his traveling companions nodded in agreement as Paul's words found the page.

What did they set out to write?

Letters

Who did they write this letter to?
The church in Thessalonica. Paul, Silas, and Timothy brought the gospel to Thessalonica during Paul's second missionary journey. The resulting church contained some Jews and many Gentiles.

Why did they write to the Thessalonians?

To inspire hope and encourage holiness | Paul, Silas, and Timothy worried about the young church. They loved them as family and longed for their new faith to flourish. But the evangelists had seen firsthand the persecution that hounded the new church. Timothy brought word that the persecution had escalated and that while the new Christians had shown steadfastness in living a Christian life, they had some misconceptions about the final return of Jesus Christ. Paul, along with Silas and Timothy, wrote to revitalize the Thessalonians vision of their God who promises to redeem his world and sustain his people.

When did they write to the Thessalonians?

AD 50 or 51 | Paul, Silas, and Timothy left Thessalonica in a hurry. Paul went on to spread the gospel in Barea, Athens, and Corinth where he wrote his letters to the Thessalonians only a few months after having left them by night. The letters are believed to have been written between AD 50 or 51 making 1 Thessalonians either Paul's first or second letter and some of the earliest written words of the whole New Testament.

What was Thessalonica like?

A Thriving Metropolis | Thessalonica was the capital of the province of Macedonia making it politically significant to Rome. The city had proven itself a partner to the Roman Empire and been granted the title of a "free city," which allowed the local municipality to enjoy support from Rome without the strict oversight and requirements placed on other cities under Roman rule.

As a port city along the Aegean Sea and a major roadway—the via Egnatia—the city displayed rich cultural and religious diversity. The community leaned Greek but boasted a multi-ethnic population with a variety of religious influences. Worship of Greek gods, Egyptian gods, Phrygian gods, and adherence to the Imperial cult, which worshiped Caesar as divine, could be found throughout Thessalonica. In addition, traveling teachers brought new philosophies and declarations of divinity as they passed through the city. On the whole, Thessalonica cultivated a lively political, cultural, religious, and social scene.

PREPARE

These letters to the Thessalonians continue the story of Paul's time with the church that sprang up while he was in Thessalonica. Before you open 1 and 2 Thessalonians, prepare for your study by reading the account of Paul, Silas, and Timothy in Thessalonica recorded in **Acts 17:1–15**. Familiarize yourself with the story and take the time to note any details that feel important.

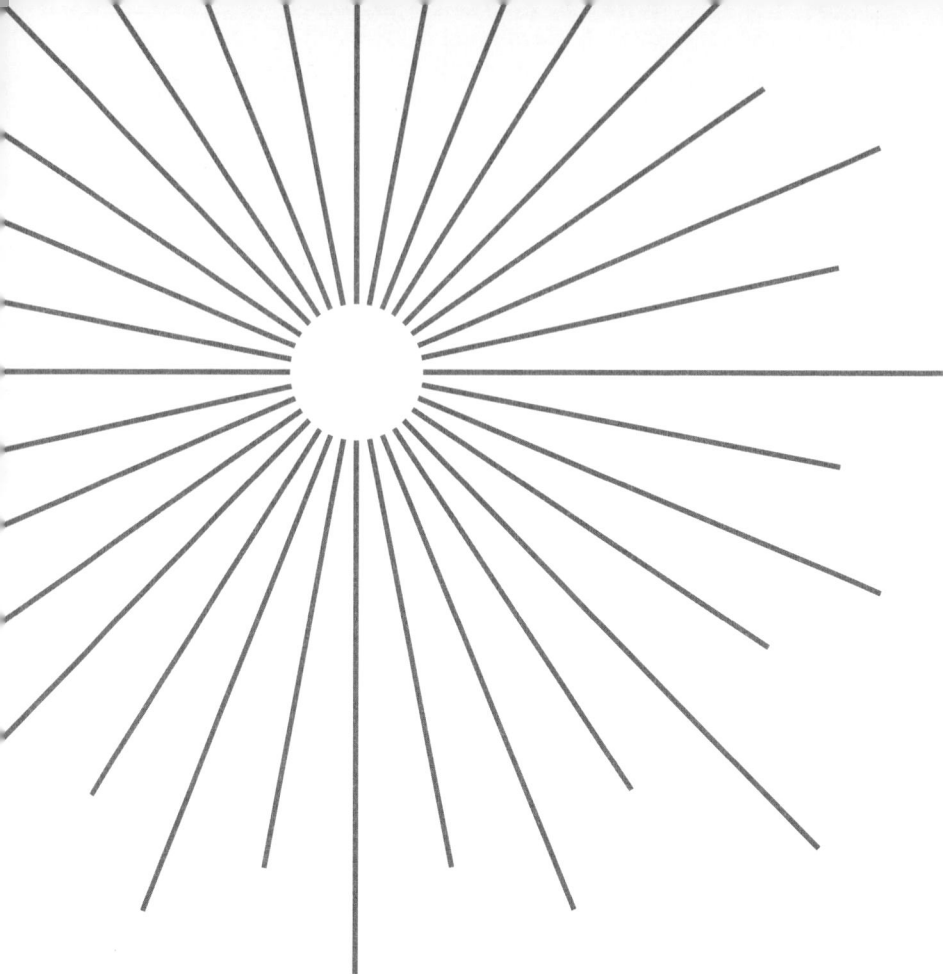

Hope

Viewing our present life through the lens of God's certain promises for the future

Holiness

God's people acting in a way that pleases him

The Family of God

The bond of love, appreciation, and care between all people in the community of believers

Hope
Viewing our present life through
the lens of God's certain
promises for the future

Holiness
God's people acting in a way
that pleases him

The Family of God
The bond of love, appreciation,
and care between all people in
the community of believers

The Return of Jesus Christ

The day the Lord Jesus Christ returns to earth fulfilling God's promise to put the world right through his judgment, mercy, grace, and eternal presence

God's Faithfulness

The sure and certain actions of God to save, sustain, and sanctify his people

THEMES

The Return of Jesus Christ

The day the Lord Jesus Christ returns to earth fulfilling God's promise to put the world right through his judgment, mercy, grace, and eternal presence

God's Faithfulness

The sure and certain actions of God to save, sustain, and sanctify his people

You Welcomed the Message

1 THESSALONIANS 1:2–10

We open up Paul's letter to find the apostle and his partners in ministry overcome with gratitude and affection. The gospel message they brought to the city hadn't just been accepted by a group of Thessalonians—it had changed them in an undeniable way. Paul, Silas, and Timothy knew the only plausible explanation for the faith, love, and hope of these new believers was the powerful work of the Holy Spirit in and among them. Remembering all the Lord had done led them to give thanks that the Thessalonians had surely become children of the day.

GET FAMILIAR WITH THE WORDS ON THE PAGE.

1 THESSALONIANS 1:2–10

READ

The foundation of every Bible study is comprehension. Read the entire book of **1 Thessalonians** and then pick different methods for intentionally reading through this week's section of verses.

You'll find a log in the back of your book to keep track of the number of times and ways you have read large sections or the entire book(s) of **1 and 2 Thessalonians**.

STUDY SKILL | READ INTENTIONALLY

We have all been guilty of reading something from start to finish only to realize we have no idea what it said. There are ways to force ourselves to engage our intellect while we read and increase our comprehension. Here are some options that will help your repetitive reading result in comprehension:

Read with a pen in hand. Mark your observations as you go. Print a double-spaced copy of **1 and 2 Thessalonian**s to mark up and make notes on as you read.

Read the same text in different translations. None of the Bible was written in English. Translators do the hard work of translating multiple copies of the original ancient Hebrew, ancient Greek, and ancient Aramaic into modern English. Seeing how different translations of the Bible render the original words will broaden your understanding of the text and highlight details you didn't notice in your standard translation.

Listen to the text. Listening to someone else read can help you hear things you didn't notice on your own and open your imagination to tone and change of characters. There are lots of great audio Bibles out there as well as apps like Streetlights for listening to the Bible.

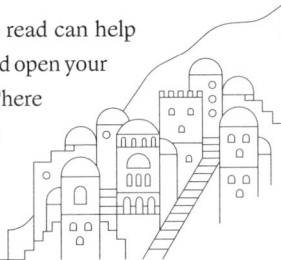

OBSERVE

Write down some details you noticed during your reading and rereading making sure to include where you see the main themes addressed in this section. The list of things to look for is always in the introduction if you need a reminder. Make a goal to list at least twenty observations.

QUESTION

Reading for detail and listing your observations can jump start your intellect. Lean into your curiosity and write down questions or subjects you'd like to understand better in this week's text

WORK THROUGH THIS WEEK'S TEXT VERSE BY VERSE. ———————

STUDY IT

1. The letter begins with a prayer of thanksgiving.

Who thanks God?_____

When do they thank God? _____

Who do they thank God for?_____

How often do they mention them in their

prayers? _____

Look at **1:2** and write down what you learn from the prayer.

2. According to the beginning of **verse 3**, what activity do Paul, Silas, and Timothy initiate in the presence of God?

3. What three traits of genuine faith do Paul, Silas, and Timothy recall in the presence of God?

4. The combination of faith, hope, and love became a signature of Paul's teaching. You can find iterations of this triad in his letters to the Corinthians, the Romans, and the Colossians, among others. Here in **1 Thessalonians**, each trait is individually coupled with a description of how it's practiced.

Below each virtue note how Paul, Silas, and Timothy describe the way faith, love, and hope are put into action. The first is completed as an example.

Faith	Love	Hope
works		

5. Look up the following verses and notice how they deepen your understanding of **verse 3**.

James 2:14–18

Ephesians 4:1–5

Romans 5:1–5

Theology Primer

The doctrine of election has been the source of more debate than we could possibly summarize here. But at its core, the central idea of election is the affirmation that salvation is the work of God. Beginning in Genesis, God chooses Abraham (Genesis 12:1–3) as the recipient of his covenant promises. Then he goes on to choose Israel as his people (Exodus 19:5–6). God choosing or electing his people clearly continues into the New Testament (Ephesians 1:3–6; 1 Peter 2:9–10).

The Bible consistently focuses the basis of God's choice on a singular quality—love. God elects simply because he loves us (Deuteronomy 7:7–8). Often throughout the scriptures, you can see God's choice tied to or put in close proximity to his love. In 1 Thessalonians 1:4 the two are connected: "For we know, brothers and sisters loved by God, that he has chosen you."

Much of the conversation around election concerns how election works. While that's important for us to think about, we also need to know how the Bible talks about election. Instead of introducing election in order to explain the ins and outs of God's choice, the Bible broaches the topic to build up the people of God. Election is mentioned to provide assurance of salvation, elicit praise, confirm the identity of God's people, call God's people into holiness, and increase joy.

FOLLOW THE LOGIC

6. Let's take a minute to track the authors' line of logic in **verses 3–5**. Start by filling in the blanks below. After you fill in the blanks, highlight or circle the first word in **verses 4** and **5** (as a reminder, scripture references come from the CSB version of the bible).

Why did the Thessalonians exhibit such noteworthy faith, hope, and love?

"_____we know, brothers and sisters _____by _____, that he has _____ you" (**v. 4**).

How do Paul, Silas, and Timothy know the Thessalonians are loved and chosen by God?

"_____our gospel did _____ come to you in _____ _____, but also in _____, in the _____, and with full_____" (**v. 5**).

7. Which of the following describes the kind of statement **verse 4** makes about the Thessalonian church:

_____ A statement of identity (who they are)

_____ A statement of purpose (what they should do)

_____ A statement of value (what they are worth)

8. Which of the following describes the kind of statement **verse 5** makes about Paul, Silas, and Timothy's certainty?

_____ A statement of theory (a possible reason)

_____ A statement of proof (a verifiable experience)

_____ A statement of assumption (a belief without proof)

"For Paul, remembering was a kind of spiritual discipline."

Nijay K. Gupta, *1–2 Thessalonians: A New Covenant Commentary*

9. Thinking back to what we learned about the Thessalonian church in Part 1, why might Paul, Silas, and Timothy choose to begin their letter by addressing the Thessalonians with thanksgiving and a reminder of their true identity as those chosen and deeply loved by God?

10. In **1:5**, Paul, Silas, and Timothy remind the Thessalonians of the manner in which the gospel message was proclaimed to them. What made this preaching unique? Who do they credit for that experience? Look up **Ephesians 6:17**. What does it add to your understanding of this description?

11. Now rewrite **verse 5** in your own words. Try to capture the unique force and conviction of Paul, Silas, and Timothy's gospel proclamation.

12. Paul, Silas, and Timothy's powerful teaching had a profound impact on the Thessalonians. According to **1:6**, what else about the evangelists impacted the Thessalonians and how did they respond?

13. In what specific way do the Thessalonians imitate those who brought them the gospel message?

14. This is the second time in two verses that the authors have mentioned a work of the Holy Spirit.

    Fill in the chart with the blessings the Holy Spirit has distributed to God's people.

	The recipient	What the Holy Spirit gave them
1:5		
1:6		

15. Joy, power, and assurance were given to God's people by the Holy Spirit. What does that mean about those characteristics?

    ____ They are characteristic of God

    ____ They are characteristics of God's kingdom

    ____ They are characteristics of both God and his kingdom

16. The opening verses of 1 Thessalonians make it clear that God and his kingdom are marked by joy, power, and assurance. Which of those characteristics is easiest for you to believe and celebrate? Which is the hardest to believe and celebrate? Why?

"Wherever the gospel goes and people respond, there is joy—joy in heaven among the angels over sinners repenting, as Jesus said, and joy on earth among the people of God."

John R. W. Stott, *The Message of 1 & 2 Thessalonians*

17. Now look at **1:7**. The Thessalonians were first imitators, but what did they become next? And what was the result?

18. Think back to what we learned in Part 1 about the city of Thessalonica. What characteristics of the city made it a strategic choice for accelerating the spread of the gospel message?

19. The testimony of the Thessalonian church spread far and wide moving at a pace faster than Paul and his companions could match. Look up **Joshua 2:8–11**. Where else has the reputation of God preceded the arrival of his people? Who was ready to receive the messengers and their proclamation because of it? What did they know about God because of what they heard?

20. In what ways does the report of Paul, Silas, and Timothy in **1:6–10** follow the pattern of the story in Joshua?

21. The testimony of the Thessalonians' conversion is made up of three parts. Complete each of the following statements then underline the action in each step.

Turned Away From	
Intentionally Served	
Waited Patiently For	

22. The Thessalonians' actions aligned with the story of scripture. How is the story of scripture reflected in the Thessalonians' testimony of turning from idols, serving Jesus Christ, and waiting for his return?

23. Looking back over the first chapter we can see that Paul, Silas, and Timothy have praised a pattern of evangelism that played out among the Thessalonians. Fill in the sequence with the reference to the corresponding verse. Then label each box either "Proclamation" or "Reception."

> The gospel came to the Thessalonians.
> **1 Thess 1:**_____
>
> |
>
> They welcomed the gospel message.
> **1 Thess 1:** _____
>
> |
>
> The gospel message rang out from them.
> **1 Thess 1:** _____

24. Read the Great Commission in **Matthew 28:16–20** and Jesus's words to his disciples in **Acts 1:8**. How does the pattern we see play out in Thessalonica reflect the plan of God to bring the gospel news of Jesus the Christ and the kingdom of God to the whole earth?

WRAP-UP

25. Now that you have studied **1 Thessalonians 1:2–10**, write a short summary of the verses in your own words. Then identify how this text rehearses, explains, or reveals a part of the story of scripture or the entire story of scripture.

APPLY IT

PERSONAL

Take some time to consider your own story. What feelings does remembering your conversion stir in you?

What part of your old life have you left behind to serve God even though it was difficult? Is there a faithfulness of God or experience of the Christian life that made it worth the work? How can remembering the past help you leave behind something else that you need to turn from?

Where have you seen the Holy Spirit clearly bestow gifts of joy, power, and conviction to someone around you? In what ways were the character of God and his kingdom revealed to you in that moment? What can you do to make a habit of telling people the work of God in and among them for the sake of their encouragement?

COMMUNAL

Paul, Silas, and Timothy described the Thessalonian church as a whole exhibiting a faith that works, a love that labors, and a hope that endures. In what ways do these three virtues accurately describe your church community? In what ways does your community fail to live up to the praise given to the Thessalonians?

Can you identify a person in your own community (not popular figures you don't typically interact with) whose Christian life you'd like to imitate? What would change about your life if you intentionally looked to imitate that person?

UNIVERSAL

Has your personal experience of salvation become a private memory instead of a public confession? In what areas of your life can you follow the lead of the Thessalonians and ensure the gospel message rings out from you wherever you go?

Turning from constant idol worship had the Thessalonians' neighbors talking. What clear signs of following Jesus Christ would get your neighbors talking about your faith?

Live Worthy of God

In chapter 1, Paul, Silas, and Timothy remembered how God had transformed the Thessalonians into faithful Christians. Now they recall how they acted in faithfulness to God and to the gospel that they brought to Thessalonica. In the ancient world, traveling teachers and sage-for-pay hucksters moved from city to city offering wisdom and magic for their own gain and everyone else's loss. Paul's words assure the church he cherishes that there is no reason to doubt his message or any evidence that he, Silas, or Timothy came as conmen. Their behavior not only proved their authenticity, but also became an example to the often persecuted Thessalonians of how to live a life worthy of the God to whom they belong.

GET FAMILIAR WITH THE WORDS ON THE PAGE. ———————————

1 THESSALONIANS 2:1–16

READ

Continue using the reading log in the back of your book to keep track of the number of times and ways you have read large sections or the entire book(s) of **1 and 2 Thessalonians**.

OBSERVE

Write down some details you noticed during your reading and rereading making sure to include where you see the main themes addressed in this section. Remember, the goal is to list at least twenty observations.

QUESTION

Indulge your curiosity and write down your questions about the Bible text.

STUDY IT

1. Read 1 Thessalonians 2:1–2. In verse 2, Paul mentions the way he, Silas, and Timothy were treated in two different places. What are the cities and how does he describe their treatment?

City #1: _____

Description of their treatment:

_____

City #2: _____

Description of their treatment:

_____

2. The original audience would have been familiar with the stories behind those simple descriptions, but we likely need to refresh our memories. Look up what **Acts 16:6-40** reports about Paul, Silas, and Timothy's time in Phillipi and what **Acts 17:1-10** reports about their time in Thessalonica. Write a basic sequence of events from their arrival to their departure.

	Phillipi	Thessalonica
Arrival •		•
Exit •		•

3. After their treatment in Philippi, how would you expect Paul, Silas, and Timothy to approach their ministry in Thessalonica? According to **2:2**, how did they actually approach their ministry in Thessalonica?

What made this possible? Was it just a personality trait?

*Make no mistake when reading this celebration of endurance amidst suffering—we are not called to endure abuse. There are many instances in the New Testament where Paul and other Christians endure physical beatings and continue on in their ministries. None of these are meant to encourage anyone to stay in a situation where they are physically abused or beaten. The Bible clearly denounces physical abuse and Paul does so himself by publicly denouncing the abuse he suffered in Philippi (**Acts 16:37**). If you are being physically abused or beaten, seek safety, find help, and report your abuser to the authorities. Our mighty God of justice is for you and with you. You can find help and report the abuse through the National Domestic Violence Hotline at 1-800-799-7233 or your state's Domestic Violence Hotline.*

4. In **verses 3–7**, Paul defends and explains the ministry he, Silas, and Timothy had among the Thessalonians. Look closely at **verse 3**. In the blanks write the three things that did not characterize the evangelists. Then circle whether it's a defense of their message, motives, or method.

   "For our exhortation didn't come from..." (1:3)

   1. _____
   Defense of their:
   Message   Method   Motives

   2. _____
   Defense of their:
   Message   Method   Motives

   3. _____
   Defense of their:
   Message   Method   Motives

5. What proof does Paul offer in **verses 4** and **5** that their message is authentic, their motives pure, and their methods upright?

Proof of:	
Authentic Message (**2:4a**)	
Pure Motives (**2:4b–5**)	
Upright Methods (**2:5–6**)	

6. According to **2:5**, what two parties does Paul say can confirm his claims?

"Nursing a baby is vitally different from a sexual act, but it too is a true commingling of two people in mutual vulnerability and dependence. New Testament Christians are seen sharing their resources, living communally, bearing one another's burdens, loving each other deeply, and expressing love physically."

Rebecca McLaughlin, *Confronting Christianity*

7. In **verse 7**, Paul begins to emphasize that they did more than just act morally in Thessalonica. Fill in the blanks in the verse to show what they avoided and what they chose to be instead.

"Although we could have been a_____ as Christ's apostles, instead we were _____ among you, as a nurse nurtures her own children." (**1:7**)

8. Paul, like all of the biblical authors thoughtfully chose the images he used. Read back through **2:7–12** and note the two familial roles Paul applies to himself and his counterparts.

First image _____

Second image _____

9. Look at **verse 8**. How does Paul explain the way in which he, Silas, and Timothy act as a nursing mother would?

Make a list of the characteristics of a nursing mother displayed in this description. In what practical ways do you think the three men lived this way among the Thessalonians?

10. In **verse 9**, Paul gives an example of how they gave of their own selves to keep from being a burden. Read the verses and then note how they clarify the example that Paul is giving.

1 Corinthians 9:14 | What could Paul have asked of the Thessalonians?_____

_____

Acts 20:34–35 | What kind of burden are they relieving by working night and day? _____

_____

Acts 18:3 | What kind of work is Paul likely doing?

_____

_____

11. In **verse 10**, Paul calls again on the Thessalonians and God as witnesses. What are they witnesses to?

12. Having already said he cared for them as a mother, he now emphasizes that he cared for them as a father. How does Paul explain the way in which he, Silas, and Timothy acts as a father in **verses 11 and 12**?

Make a list of the characteristics of a father displayed in this description. In what practical ways do you think the three men may have lived this way among the Thessalonians?

13. The crescendo of **verse 12** is at the very end. What is Paul's greatest desire for the Thessalonian church?

14. Keeping in mind all we've learned in the first two chapters of 1 Thessalonians, how do we know Paul is not telling the Thessalonians they must earn their way into God's kingdom?

FOLLOW THE LOGIC

15. Fill in the chart below to see the line of thinking in **2:13–14** that leaves Paul overcome with gratitude.

> **Why do Paul, Silas, and Timothy thank God?**
>
> "This is why we constantly thank God, because when you _____
>
> the _____ of _____ that you heard from us, you_____
>
> _____ not as a human message, but as it _____ _____" **(v. 13a)**.
>
> **What is changing the Thessalonians?**
>
> "the _____ of _____ , which also _____ _____
>
> in you _____ _____" **(v. 13b)**.
>
> **What evidence does Paul give that the Thessalonian believers are being changed?**
>
> "For you, brothers and sisters, _____ _____of _____
>
> _____ in Christ Jesus that are in Judea, since you have _____
>
> _____ the same things from people of your own country, just
>
> as they did from the Jews" **(v. 14)**.

16. Look up **Philippians 1:27–29**. How do those verses help you understand what Paul says and why he says it in **2:10–14**?

> "Whatever the importance of the apostles and their labor, God is now active among the Thessalonians themselves. The apostles have been and will continue to be significant for them, but it is also the case that God works among them directly, just as God chose them in the beginning."
>
> Beverly Roberts Gaventa, *First and Second Thessalonians*

*Bible readers throughout history have wrestled with Paul's words in **2:14–16**. Without paying attention specifically to what Paul is and isn't saying and without considering his vast catalogue of writing, people have used this text to justify anti-Semitic thoughts and behaviors. We want to be clear from the outset that there are no grounds in these verses—or any other Bible text—to justify anti-Judaism in any form or fashion.*

The questions that follow intend to guide you in deciphering what Paul is communicating to the Thessalonian church (and all believers) and to help you see that he is neither demonstrating nor advocating for any prejudice.

STUDY SKILL | READING THE BIBLE IN CONTEXT

The Bible is one of the greatest resources we have for understanding the Bible. One of the strongest temptations for any student of the scriptures is to take what they are reading out of context. The beautiful and astounding reality of our Bibles is that everything in them is meant to meld together, not stand alone.

When we arrive at a text that is hard to understand, we need more context. A helpful approach is to work through the context of what is being said from its most narrow to its most broad categories. Students of the scriptures should ask: how do these words fit in these verses, this chapter, this book, this testament, and the story of scripture?

Let's use the method described in the study skill section to make sense of Paul's words in **2:14–16**.

VERSES ———————————————————————————————

17. What characterizes the group Paul is speaking about in **2:14–16?** Circle all that apply.

    Jewish

    Killed the Lord Jesus

    Persecuted Paul and his co-laborers

    Oppose the spread of the gospel

    Displease God

    Hostile to everyone

18. These people stand in the way of the gospel reaching:

    ____ Themselves

    ____ Others the evangelists try to speak to

19. The antagonizing actions toward the gospel message and God are:

    ____ A one-time event

    ____ A continuous pattern

CHAPTERS ———————————————————————————————

20. What place do these verses have in Paul's argument that he, Silas, and Timothy taught the Thessalonians by example and by word how to live worthy of God?

BOOK

21. How does Paul pointing out that the Thessalonians' faithfulness to God amidst persecution reinforce the purpose of his letter?

TESTAMENT

Read the following two verses and then answer the questions below:

Acts 17:1–3

"*After they passed through Amphipolis and Apollonia, they came to Thessalonica, where there was a Jewish synagogue. As usual, Paul went into the synagogue, and on three Sabbath days reasoned with them from the Scriptures, explaining and proving that it was necessary for the Messiah to suffer and rise from the dead: "This Jesus I am proclaiming to you is the Messiah."*"

Romans 9:1–5

"*I speak the truth in Christ—I am not lying; my conscience testifies to me through the Holy Spirit— that I have great sorrow and unceasing anguish in my heart. For I could wish that I myself were cursed and cut off from Christ for the benefit of my brothers and sisters, my own flesh and blood. They are Israelites, and to them belong the adoption, the glory, the covenants, the giving of the law, the temple service, and the promises. The ancestors are theirs, and from them, by physical descent, came the Christ, who is God over all, praised forever. Amen*"

22. Where does Paul typically go first when bringing the gospel to a new city?

_____ City center
_____ Jewish synagogue
_____ Homes of friends and family

23. What does Paul do when he arrives at the synagogue:

_____ Announces the wrath of God
_____ Uses the Jewish scriptures to prove that Jesus is the Messiah promised to the Jews

24. What is Paul's greatest hope for his fellow Jews?

_____ That they would be saved
_____ That they would know God's wrath

25. On a scale of 1 to 10 how passionate does Paul seem about the salvation of his own people, the Jews?

1   2   3   4   5   6   7   8   9   10

26. With your contextual study of these verses in mind, we can conclude with confidence that Paul was speaking about:

_____ All Jewish people throughout all of time
_____ Specific group of Jewish people who had actively rejected the gospel and continually acted in hostility against God

27. In what ways do you think the Thessalonians suffering is comparable to the suffering of the Judean churches? What is Paul's intended purpose in pointing out the similarities in **2:14-16**?

28. In what ways should the Christian community be an obvious contrast to the persecutors described in **2:14–16**? What is Paul's intended purpose in pointing out the differences?

29. You've read through the whole book of **1 Thessalonians** twice, but take another quick look at the end of the book, specifically **5:23–24**. What enables the Thessalonians to accomplish the seemingly overwhelming task Paul asks of them?

WRAP-UP

30. Now that you have studied **1 Thessalonians 2:1–16**, write a short summary of the verses in your own words. Then identify how this text rehearses, explains, or reveals a part of the story of scripture or the entire story of scripture.

APPLY IT

PERSONAL

Paul has called the Thessalonians to live a life worthy of the glorious kingdom of God. Are you prone to forget that this is possible only by the power of God and in community? How can you regularly remind yourself God doesn't expect you to simply muscle your way to obedience?

Paul and those with him show us an extensive example of leadership, some of which runs counter to the standard way we think of leaders acting. What counter-cultural aspect of leadership exhibited here can you ask the Lord to develop in you?

For the Thessalonian church, conforming to a way of life that was worthy of God meant refusing to conform to a way of life offered to them by their unbelieving society. What ways of society do you need to reject in order to conform to a way of life worthy of God?

COMMUNAL

Paul tells us that he, Silas, and Timothy shared their own lives with the Thessalonians, which is as an example of how we are to live with one another. Who have you chosen to share your whole life with? What fruit of faithfulness has come from it? How can you further follow Paul, Silas, and Timothy's example in this way?

We are prone to think of our suffering as unique to ourselves, but Paul tells us differently. Can you make a list of those who have faithfully suffered in a comparable way to your current suffering or ways in which you've suffered previously? How does their companionship and example encourage you?

Can you make a list of the ways you have seen the Word of God work effectively in your Christian community?

UNIVERSAL

Paul's example of leadership shows gentleness, sacrifice, affection, care, love, education, protection, and modeling the way to live a citizen of God's kingdom. Where have you seen Christian leaders fall short of Paul's standard? How did that affect the society around them? What about leaders who have followed Paul's example of leadership? How does that affect the society around them?

NOTES

04

For Now We Live

1 THESSALONIANS 2:17–3:13

Paul, Silas, and Timothy's time in Thessalonica ended abruptly. A quick escape under the cover of darkness in order to flee an angry mob doesn't leave much time for explanations or goodbyes. Paul assures the Thessalonians that he, Silas, and Timothy felt the pain of the sudden separation as acutely as the Thessalonian Christians. But out of sight certainly didn't mean out of mind. Paul thought of his new family in Thessalonica so often that he couldn't go without knowing how they were doing and making certain they had someone to instruct and encourage them in their new faith. This turned out to be as good for Paul, Silas, and Timothy as it was for the Thessalonians.

GET FAMILIAR WITH THE WORDS ON THE PAGE.

1 THESSALONIANS 2:17-3:13

KNOW IT

READ

Continue using the reading log in the back of your book to keep track of the number of times and ways you have read large sections or the entire book(s) of 1 and 2 Thessalonians.

OBSERVE

Write down some details you noticed during your reading and rereading making sure to include where you see the main themes addressed in this section. Remember, the goal is at least twenty observations.

QUESTION

Indulge your curiosity and write down your questions about the Bible text.

STUDY IT

WORK THROUGH THIS WEEK'S TEXT VERSE BY VERSE.

1. What is the first word of **2:17**? What contrast in content and tone does Paul create between **2:14–16** and **2:17–20**?

    First Word: _____

2:14–16		2:17–20
	versus	

2. Did Paul and his co-laborers leave the city voluntarily?

    Considering how Paul cherished the Thessalonians, how do you think he and his companions felt about having to leave them?

3. According to **2:17**, did Paul, Silas, and Timothy forget the Thessalonians after they were forced out of the city?

4. What reason does Paul give for being unable to return to the Thessalonians?

    Think back over **chapters 1 and 2**. Why would Satan have a vested interest in keeping Paul and the Thessalonians apart?

5. Paul's praise becomes profusive in **verses 18 and 19**. List every description Paul gives of what the Thessalonians mean to him, Silas, and Timothy.

6. That's a lot of love. Read Paul's words in **Philippians 2:13–18**. What do they add to your understanding of why Paul's love for Thessalonians was so deep?

7. At this point, Paul introduces a theme that will continue to build throughout this letter and **2 Thessalonians** as well. Fill in the blanks of **verse 19** to identify the theme.

    "For who is our hope or joy or crown of boasting in the _____ of our _____ _____ at his _____? Is it not you?" (**2:19**)

8. Which of the following describes how Paul feels about the coming day of the Lord (the return of Jesus)? Check all that apply.

    ____ Worried   ____ Scared

    ____ Eager   ____ Anxious

    ____ Confident

> "Each of us has our own work of love to perform, whether it be quiet and secret or well known and public."
>
> N.T. Wright, *Paul for Everyone: Galatians and Thessalonians*

9. Paul's statement of love and his desire to see the Thessalonians moves into action in **chapter 3**. According to **3:1–2**, how did Paul deal with Satan's attempt to outwit him?

    Did Paul, Silas, or Timothy have any assurance that their plan would work when they implemented it?

10. Paul gives Timothy two titles in **3:2**. What are they? What does this tell you about how Paul thought about his ministry partners and the kind of leadership Paul exhibited?

    Timothy's Titles

    1.   2.

Theology Primer

The story of scripture ends with God redeeming all of creation from sin and suffering and putting the world right through his judgment, mercy, grace, and eternal presence. In the narrative of scripture God actively accomplishes his promised end in two parts.

Part one has two components: the first arrival of Jesus Christ and God sending his Spirit to dwell among believers. In Jesus's arrival, life, death, resurrection, and ascension God begins to accomplish the redemption he promised in the earliest pages of the Old Testament. After Jesus ascends to heaven, God sends the Spirit to the newly created church to be the personal presence of God among his people and a guarantee of the complete fulfillment of God's promised redemption. After these events, God's promises are being fulfilled but only in part. Suffering still abounds in the world. The effects of sin in each Christian's life and in the world are undeniable. Death comes for all without exception. Part one alone does not bring the redemption of all things. It brings a hint of that redemption and a guarantee of its completion, but God has promised a part two that Paul and other authors of the Bible speak about throughout their writings.

In part two, Jesus Christ returns and the Spirit completes the work of transformation. The return of Jesus will be a physical return just as our Savior's first arrival was physical. When Jesus returns, the kingdom of God will fully vanquish the kingdom of earth and the Son of God will deal out judgment toward God's enemies and mercy toward his church. On that day, creation and God's people—both those who have died and those who are alive at the time—will be fully redeemed and will reign over the earth full of the glory and knowledge of God. This is the day Paul looks toward in the books of 1 and 2 Thessalonians when he speaks about the coming of the Lord Jesus.

FOLLOW THE LOGIC

11. Let's follow Paul's logic again, this time in **3:2–5**.

What did Paul send Timothy to do in Thessalonica?

*"And we sent Timothy, our brother and God's coworker in the gospel of Christ, to _____ and _____ you _____your _____" (**v. 2**).*

What was the goal of Timothy's time in Thessalonica?

*"So that ____ _____ will be_____ by these_____" (**v. 3a**).*

Why did the Thessalonians need this kind of support from Timothy?

*"In fact, when we were with you, we _____ _____in _____ that we were going to _____ _____, and as you know, _____ _____" (**v. 4**).*

12. Paul reminds his dearly loved friends and new Christian converts that living a faithful Christian life would mean they faced persecution because of their faith. Look up the following verses and note who also taught this message and how it expands your understanding of this teaching.

Matt. 5:11–12	
1 Peter 4:12–13	
Psalm 102:1–2	

13. Continue on to **3:5**. What was Paul's greatest fear for the Thessalonians during his unplanned absence from them?

14. If anyone knows about the possible effects of "affliction," it is Paul. In our study so far, we have read some of the stories of his many sufferings and persecution. What kind of affliction might Paul have in mind that would be so powerful? Describe at least one example for each category.

	Example
Economic Affliction	
Physical Affliction	
Mental Affliction	
Spiritual Affliction	

15. Why would Paul prioritize teaching that suffering is likely coming for believers?

16. Now look at **3:6**. What did Timothy report when he returned? Were Paul's worst fears confirmed or alleviated?

17. What two categories did Timothy bring good news about? What did the Thessalonians hope for? What triad of attributes does this remind you of from **1:3**?

18. One reason Timothy was sent to Thessalonica was to encourage the believers in their faith. How have the tables turned in **3:7**?

19. Paul has made it abundantly clear to the Thessalonians that his own joy is bound up with theirs. How does he take that idea even further in **verse 8**?

What two familial images from **chapter 2** does this statement reflect?

"So filled to the brim with joy is Paul at this [good] news that he could not possibly think of a big enough gift to give back to God for God's gift of the Thessalonians to him."

Nijay K. Gupta, *1–2 Thessalonians: A New Covenant Commentary*

20. Paul's joy in **verses 6–8** overflows in **verse 9** into even more thanksgiving for the faithfulness of the Thessalonians. Who does Paul thank? What does that tell us about who he attributes their continued faithfulness to?

21. What two things does Paul pray for as part of his thanksgiving in **verse 10**?

1. _____

2. _____

22. Up until this point, Paul has given us no reason to believe there is any flaw to find in the Thessalonians' faith. To help us understand Paul's statement, mark the following statements true or false.

T	F	
		At the time Paul is writing, the Thessalonian church is still a new, young church.
		Paul had plenty of time with the Thessalonians to teach them all they needed to know and to answer all their questions.
		Paul's joy is found in the Thessalonians' happiness, not the strength of their faith.
		Paul believes that the word of God will continue to work effectively in the Thessalonians over time.

23. Does Paul's statement about completing "what is lacking in your faith" contradict any of the praise he has previously lavished on the Thessalonians for their faith?

24. Read Paul's prayer in **3:11–13**. What does Paul include in his vision for the Thessalonian church? How does he believe these things can come to be?

	What Paul prays for the church	How it can be accomplished
3:11		
3:12		
3:13		

25. Read through the prayer one more time and list the attributes of God you see exhibited in Paul's words. Use the attributes list in appendix C on page 154 to help with your answer.

WRAP-UP

26. Now that you have studied **1 Thessalonians 2:17–3:13**, write a short summary of the verses in your own words. Then identify how this text rehearses, explains, or reveals a part of the story of scripture or the entire story of scripture.

APPLY IT

THESE QUESTIONS ARE JUST TO GET YOU STARTED.
THIS SPACE IS OPEN FOR ANY REFLECTION AND APPLICATION.

PERSONAL

Do you believe God's faithfulness will result in an absence of trials? How do Paul's words correct, encourage, and give you hope?

How do you react when you feel hindered from accomplishing what God has called you to? Are you prone to wave the white flag or do you actively try to find a way around the hindrance? Is there a hindrance in your life now that has left you ready to quit? How can you revive your energy to keep looking for a workaround?

How does it encourage you to know that you will personally grow over time and that good leaders will find joy in your growth? How does it make you feel about the areas where you feel "lacking in your faith"?

COMMUNAL

Paul and his co-laborers choose to entwine their lives with the Thessalonians. Has your church or faith community decided to intentionally open up their lives to one another? Do you harbor beliefs about privacy, individualism, family, or personality type that keep others at a distance instead of drawing them in?

How does it encourage you to know that your church and faith community will grow over time and that good leaders will find joy in that growth? How does it make you feel about the areas where your church or faith community feel "lacking in your faith"?

UNIVERSAL

If you were to live out the kind of love Paul is expressing here, how would the community around you respond? Would they think you were crazy? Would you draw attention? Would they want to be a part of the community they saw in action?

Use your gospel imagination for a minute. What kind of gospel change could happen in the world if we decided to actively work around hindrances that keep us from seeing God's kingdom established on earth? What injustices might we eradicate? What people might be given a new hope in the midst of despair? What new opportunities for bringing the kingdom of God to earth might arise if we used what was at our disposal right now in a new way? Try to be specific with your answers.

NOTES

05

Please God Even More

1 THESSALONIANS 4:1–18

At this point in the letter, an encouraged Paul takes up the role of instructor. The Thessalonians have relied on the Spirit of God to empower their Christian life and Paul has told them his hope and prayer is for them to abound in even more holiness. The Thessalonians want to please God and Paul wants to help them do just that. He turns to three specific areas of life where the Thessalonian church can conform to God's ways. These exhortations don't find their basis in a personal ability to obey. Rather, Paul grounds each opportunity for holiness in who God is, how God works in his people, and what God promises to do in the world.

GET FAMILIAR WITH THE WORDS ON THE PAGE. ———————————————

1 THESSALONIANS 4:1–18

READ

Continue using the reading log in the back of your book to keep track of the number of times and ways you have read large sections or the entire book(s) of 1 and 2 Thessalonians.

OBSERVE

Write down some details you noticed during your reading and rereading making sure to include where you see the main themes addressed in this section. If you need a refresh on what to look for you can revisit the list in the introduction. The goal is still at least twenty observations.

QUESTION

Indulge your curiosity and write down your questions about the Bible text.

STUDY IT

WORK THROUGH THIS WEEK'S TEXT VERSE BY VERSE.

1. **Chapter 4** marks the beginning of a new approach in Paul's letter. In the recap, place each section we have studied so far in the category it best reflects: encouragement, explanation, or instruction.

Paul remembers the Thessalonians' salvation and early faith. (**1:1–10**)	____Encouragement ____Explanation ____Instruction
Paul recounts his, Silas, and Timothy's ministry to the Thessalonians (**2:1–16**)	____Encouragement ____Explanation ____Instruction
Paul reports the events that happened after he left and reminds the Thessalonians of his love for them. (**2:17–3:13**)	____Encouragement ____Explanation ____Instruction
Paul reveals his hopes for the future of the Thessalonians' faith. (**4:1–18**)	____Encouragement ____Explanation ____Instruction

2. In **4:1**, Paul tells the Thessalonians the goal of how they should live. What does Paul describe as the goal for Christian living?

3. Look up the following verses and note the answer to each question.

John 8:29	What does Jesus say he always does?
Romans 8:8	What are those in the flesh unable to do?
2 Corinthians 5:9	What is the aim of the Christian at all times?

4. There is still more important information for us to notice in the first verse of **chapter 4**. Answer the following questions to point out those details.

Y	N	
		Are the instructions Paul lays out new to the Thessalonians?
		Have the Thessalonians made a habit of obeying these instructions?
		Have the Thessalonians exhausted all opportunities to please God?
		Are Paul's commands given in the authority of the Lord Jesus?

5. Let's think for a minute about the opportunity Christians have to increasingly please God. Read **John 10:10**. What does Jesus Christ come to provide?

How does Jesus's offer align with Paul's call for the Thessalonians to live lives that please God even more

6. Now compare the CSB translation of the beginning of **verse 3** to the NET Bible translation. Underline how each translation describes the will of God for his people.

4:3a (CSB)   For this is God's will, your sanctification.

4:3a (NET)   For this is God's will: that you become holy.

"On the other side of saving grace, we are meant to put ourselves, by whatever means possible, in the path of transformation."

Jen Pollock Michel, *Surprised by Paradox*

Theology Primer

Sanctification and holiness are important and interconnected concepts throughout the Bible. Without a doubt, Paul would have talked about these topics with the Thessalonians during his time with them. His wording in verse 3 assumes they understand the terms he is using. Let's catch up with the ancient Thessalonians and define these concepts.

The Bible describes God as "holy" more than any other term. God's holiness is a fusion of his purity and power. He is utterly good and completely powerful. And he alone is able to make everything and everyone perfect as well. (Exodus 15:11).

God's holiness is what makes him totally unique and it's also his core attribute—every other attribute of God is intertwined with his holy nature. God's love is a holy love. God's justice is a holy justice. God's mercy is a holy mercy.

Amazingly, the Bible also says that Christians can be holy. The Bible uses the word holy in relation to Christians in two ways.

The first is positional holiness, which is given to a person when they become a Christian. God sees the believer as perfectly pure because Jesus's perfect righteousness has been credited to them. Now they are set apart as children of God (John 1:12; Hebrews 10:10).

But throughout the Bible God also calls his children, who he has declared holy, to become holy. This is the second aspect of holiness—practical holiness, which is when a Christian is morally pure in their conduct (avoids sin) and reflects the character of God in all they do (pursues Christlikeness). Practical holiness means perpetually acting in a way that pleases God.

When God's people live holy lives, they are acting in accordance with the identity God has already granted them, but this doesn't happen automatically when we become Christians. We have to grow in practical holiness. That process is called sanctification. Sanctification is progressively learning to act in ways that please God.

Sanctification will never occur in our lives if we depend on our own power. And that's okay. God does not intend for us to become holy through our own strength. Practical holiness is made possible by the Holy Spirit who lives in and among God's people (Romans 15:16). In this way, God has made it possible for his children who are declared holy to become holy.

7. Paul is going to instruct the Thessalonian church on how to please God in three specific areas. **Read 4:3–7.** Circle which attribute Paul introduces and the topic he covers.

Attribute:	Topic:
Holiness	Work
Hope	Loss
Love	Sex

God's people please him by expressing

_____ in _____.

(Attribute)   (Topic)

The topic of sex often brings up shame, frustration, or memories of trauma for many people. Before you begin to work on this section, remember that Paul is speaking to a group composed of many members who had broken and difficult sexual histories and that Jesus came so that those who believe in him may have abundant life. Take a minute to pray that the Spirit of God will open your mind, soften your heart, show you his presence, and guide you into the light of his love as we approach this tender subject.

8. We often consider sex to be a personal topic. Since our bodies belong to us, we should be left to decide what we do with them, right? Paul clearly believes even the most intimate areas of our lives are to be lived in submission to God's instructions. Look up the following verses and answer the question that follows to see why Paul believes God has the ultimate authority over our lives, even when it comes to sex.

Genesis 2:7, 21–22 | Who created man and woman's bodies?

Genesis 2:24–25 | Who created sex?

1 Corinthians 6:18–20 | Who do our bodies belong to?

9. How does it make you feel that the creator God who made and designed you has authority over your body? Is it hard for you to believe that his design for sexual relationships offers you an abundant life and the joy of pleasing him?

10. Read **4:4–5** and note what should and should not characterize sexual relationships.

Act in _____

Act without _____

11. Which relational stage does Paul apply these instructions to?

___Singleness   ___Dating

___Married   ___All stages

12. What would characterize a sexual relationship that is conducted in "holiness and honor"? Look up **Proverbs 5:18–19** to help with your answer.

What does **4:4** describe as the righteous attribute that characterizes someone who acts in this manner?

13. What does Paul explicitly say in **4:6** is incompatible with a sexual relationship that is conducted in "holiness and honor"?

What does **4:5** describe as the sinful attribute that characterizes someone who acts in this manner?

14. Based on **verse 6**, how seriously does God take the sexual exploitation of another person? How should this truth incentivize self-control? How might it comfort those who have been sexually exploited?

15. In **4:7–8** Paul reiterates his main point from **4:1** and emphasizes the weight of not conforming to God's standards of holiness.

What call is reemphasized? (**4:7**)

_____

_____

If you refuse that call, who are you rejecting? (**4:8**) _____

_____

16. Let's look closer at Paul's words in **verse 8**.

If a believer in Jesus Christ rejects God's will for living a holy life, what are they rejecting?

How does Paul identify God in this context?

_____ Paul's human perspective

_____ God himself

"Consequently, anyone who rejects this does not reject man, but God, who _____ _____ his _____ _____." (**4:8**)

17. At first glance, this feels like an odd designation for Paul to make. Read the following verses and underline or highlight the role and work of the Holy Spirit.

Ephesians 1:17–19

"I pray that the God of our Lord Jesus Christ, the glorious Father, would give you the Spirit of wisdom and revelation in the knowledge of him. I pray that the eyes of your heart may be enlightened so that you may know what is the hope of his calling, what is the wealth of his glorious inheritance in the saints, and what is the immeasurable greatness of his power toward us who believe, according to the mighty working of his strength."

Ezekiel 36:25–27

"I will also sprinkle clean water on you, and you will be clean. I will cleanse you from all your impurities and all your idols. I will give you a new heart and put a new spirit within you; I will remove your heart of stone and give you a heart of flesh. I will place my Spirit within you and cause you to follow my statutes and carefully observe my ordinances."

18. Which of the following best explains Paul's reasoning for identifying God as the one who gives believers the Holy Spirit?

_____The Holy Spirit witnesses all we do and testifies to our conformity to God's commands or rejection of God's commands.

_____The Holy Spirit empowers and enables Christians to obey God's commands and please God. To reject the Holy Spirit who brings about holiness is to reject God.

_____The Holy Spirit is irrelevant in this verse.

The fact is that there is a world of difference between lust and love, between dishonourable sexual practices which use the partner and true love-making which honours the partner, between the selfish desire to possess and the unselfish desire to love, cherish and respect."

John R. W. Stott, *The Message of 1 & 2 Thessalonians*

19. Paul now switches to his second topic. Read **4:9–12.** Circle which attribute Paul introduces and the topic he covers.

Attribute:	Topic:
Holiness	Work
Hope	Loss
Love	Sex

God's people please him by expressing

_____ **in** _____ .

(Attribute)   (Topic)

20. Considering what we've just read about the Holy Spirit, how do you think the Thessalonian Christians were "taught by God" to love one another as Paul says in **4:9**?

21. Rewording Paul's instructions on work can help us understand his meaning.

Match Paul's words to the statement that best describes his intentions.

Paul's Instruction	Paul's Instruction Reworded
"Live quietly" (**4:11a**)	"Work without giving others unnecessary attention"
"Mind your own affairs" (**4:11b**)	"Find gainful employment"
"Work with your hands" (**4:11c**)	"Work without drawing unnecessary attention to yourself"

22. Look back at the example Paul, Silas, and Timothy set for how work should be approached in **2:9**. What were the two results of their approach to work while they were in Thessalonica?

How do the two results Paul cites in **chapter 2** align with the two outcomes Paul says will come from integrity in their work in **4:12**?

23. Think about what happens when someone who is able to work and who has the opportunity to work chooses not to. How is choosing to work with integrity an expression of love for others?

24. We saw in **Genesis 2** that both our physical bodies and sex are designed by our creator God. According to **Genesis 1:28** and **2:15** what responsibilities does the creator God give Adam and Eve?

The manner in which we work, like the manner in which we engage in sexual relationships, is something God has always intended to be done with holiness. How does that change the way you think about both work and sex?

25. Having given instructions for pleasing God on the topics of sex and work, Paul now switches to a third topic. Read **4:13–18**. Circle which attribute Paul introduces and the topic he covers.

Attribute:	Topic:
Holiness	Work
Hope	Loss
Love	Sex

God's people please him by expressing

_____ **in** _____.

(Attribute)　　　　　(Topic)

Like sex, death is a tender topic. Until Christ returns everyone will die a physical death, which means all of us will eventually—if we have not already—experience the profound emotional upheaval of losing someone we love. If thinking about loss causes you pain, grief, worry, or trauma, please know that Paul is lovingly addressing the anguish of the Thessalonian believers. Take a minute before moving on to ask God to encourage you and bring peace to you in the midst of your legitimate grief.

26. Look at **4:13**. What two things does Paul want to avoid? Write both "we do not want" phrases in the first column, then in the second column write what Paul implies he and his companions do want for the Thessalonian believers.

Do Not Want	Do Want
"you to be _____ brothers and sisters"	
"you will not _____ like the rest who have no hope"	

FOLLOW THE LOGIC

27. The Thessalonians have questions about the fate of their Christian loved ones who have died as well as what happens when Christ returns. Let's follow Paul's logic again, this time in **4:14–15** to see how Paul begins to answer their questions.

What example does Paul point to as proof of what will happen for all of God's people?

"For if we _____ that _____ _____ and _____ _____..." (**v. 14a**).

What does Jesus's death and resurrection mean for those who have died before Jesus returns?

"...in the_____ _____, through _____, God will_____ with_____those who have_____ _____" (**v. 14b**).

What does Jesus's death and resurrection mean for those who are alive when Jesus returns?

"For we say this to you by a word from the Lord: We who are_____ _____ at the Lord's coming will _____ _____ _____ those who have fallen asleep" (**v. 15**).

At this point Paul, not wanting the brothers and sisters to be uniformed, goes on to further explain the future return of Christ that unites all believers with each other and with Jesus Christ for eternity. He does this by laying out the progression of three events that will take place on the day of the Lord. Throughout church history people have taken a myriad of stances on the details and timeline of these events. In this section we are going to focus on what Paul does say in these two brief verses and why he chooses to communicate what he does to the grieving and worried Thessalonians.

28. In **verses 16** and **17** Paul lays out the progression of three end-times events. Write them in the blanks and note who is involved in each step.

	Event	Parties Involved
First (**4:16a**)		
Second (**4:16b**)		
Third (**4:17a**)		

29. What is the ultimate outcome of these events and what should it lead the Thessalonian church to do?

Outcome of These Events (**4:17b**)	Response of the Church (**4:18**)
Therefore	

In your own words, write out why the Thessalonians can confidently grieve with hope and encourage one another.

WRAP-UP

30. Now that you have studied **1 Thessalonians 4:1–18**, write a short summary of the verses in your own words. Then identify how this text rehearses, explains, or reveals a part of the story of scripture or the entire story of scripture.

THESE QUESTIONS ARE JUST TO GET YOU STARTED.

THIS SPACE IS OPEN FOR ANY REFLECTION AND APPLICATION.

APPLY IT

PERSONAL

In verses **1–2** Paul told us all we need to know to understand the aim of living an obedient life. Consider what Paul has said in these opening verses, then write in your own words a guiding principle for Christian living. Try to keep it to one sentence.

The sin of our hearts and the work of Satan in us and our world often flips the script that God gives us, convincing us that what God says is for our good is actually against us. What, if anything, about God's instructions for holiness in sex, love in work, and hope in death offends you? Why do you think that is? Name one person who has found joy in following God's instructions in that area and who would be willing to talk with you about your frustrations, questions, and thoughts. Ask them to encourage you to act in ways to please God even when it's hard or you don't yet understand his ways.

COMMUNAL

Paul gives Christians every reason to grieve without losing grasp of the greatest hope ever offered to humanity. Importantly, he instructs the Christian community to be the voice of God's understanding, love, and hope to one another. How have you experienced this in the midst of a tragedy? How have you offered it to someone dealing with grief? Is there a situation now where you can actively seek encouragement or actively give encouragement to grieving brothers and sisters in Christ?

All of Paul's instructions about increasingly pleasing God had a relational component. List all three topics and write out which relationships in your life would benefit from adhering to these instructions. Write one actionable step you can take within the month that would please God and strengthen the relationships you listed.

UNIVERSAL

Sex, money, and death aren't just important topics among Christians. These topics are discussed around the world. In what ways are Paul's instructions for pleasing God good news for the unbelieving community?

Do you and your Christian community feel prepared to address the Christian ethic of sex, money, and death with unbelievers in your life? Why or why not? What keeps you from speaking on these topics?

06

Children of Light

The Thessalonian Christians rightly value what God promises to do alongside what God has already done. The first coming of Jesus Christ brought their salvation and now the Thessalonian Christians live in expectation of the day Jesus will return again and God will fulfill all he promised for his people. Like every generation that came after them, the burning curiosity over when Jesus will return seems to have set in among some of the Thessalonians. Paul quickly addresses their curiosity about the timing and reframes their question. How should they live out their confidence that Jesus will return? This final chapter of Paul's letter begs the Thessalonians to live in accordance with their identity. As children of light, they should behave as those who belong to the glorious day they know is coming.

READ

This is your last week to read 1 Thessalonians. You've done great! Continue using the reading log in the back of your book to keep track of the number of times and ways you have read large sections or the entire book(s) of 1 and 2 Thessalonians.

OBSERVE

Write down some details you noticed during your reading and rereading making sure to include where you see the main themes addressed in this section. The list of things to look for is always in the introduction if you need a reminder. Make a goal to list at least twenty observations.

QUESTION

Write down some details you noticed—still shooting for twenty—during your reading and rereading making sure to include where you see the main themes addressed in this section.

KNOW IT

STUDY IT

1. What topic does Paul take up in **5:1**?

   "About the_____ and the

   _____."

Paul is addressing the timing of what event? You can look back at **4:15** to help with your answer.

You have been reading, listening to, and/or writing out this section of the book for a while now. So, you know that Paul is about to continue addressing end-times events, namely, the return of Jesus Christ. Our tendency—one seen throughout time—is to read the Bible's words on end-times events with an eye for detailed explanations of the "how." Our minds naturally draw us toward questions about God's methodology. We want to know how it will all happen and decipher clues as to when it will come about. The how of these events does matter to our faith. But if God has proved anything about how he fulfills his promises, it is that his divine imagination far surpasses our human minds. Rarely, if ever, have the fulfillments of God's promises mapped to the human estimations of how they would come about. Nowhere is this as clear as the first coming of the promised Messiah, Jesus, the Son of God. In Jesus's first coming, God both defied expectations and fulfilled every word of his promises. In our study of 1 and 2 Thessalonians our goal is to recognize what God has revealed about his methodology while connecting it to a practical theology. As these questions progress, expect to move from observing what Paul says into deciphering why he says it and what it means for us as we wait for Christ's return. By the grace of God, we will be captivated by who God is and what he will accomplish in us now and for us later.

2. Is Paul's teaching on the day of Jesus's return new? Or is it a reminder for the Thessalonians? What wording from **5:1–2** makes that evident?

3. Paul uses two metaphors to describe what the Thessalonians "know very well." Fill in the blank with the first of the two metaphors. Then read the corresponding verse to help you understand Paul's main point. Lastly, check the main idea that best fits with how Paul is using this metaphor.

   First Metaphor (5:2):

   Reference (Matthew 24:42–44)

   Main Idea:

   _____ The timing of Jesus's return will be unexpected.

   _____ Jesus's return will happen at nighttime.

   _____ Christians should be worried about the return of Jesus.

4. What will some people be saying when the time comes for Jesus to return? Look up **Ezekiel 13:10**. Why is this message a problem?

5. Now let's look at the second metaphor. Similarly, fill in the blank with the second metaphor. Then fill in the blanks of **5:3** to help you understand the main point Paul is making. Lastly, check the main idea that best fits with how Paul is using this metaphor.

   Second Metaphor (5:3):

   Reference:
   "When they say, "Peace and security," then sudden destruction will come upon them, like labor pains on a pregnant woman, and they _____ _____ _____."

   Main Idea:
   ____ The timing of Jesus's return depends on what people are saying.

   ____ Jesus's return will be painful for all people.

   ____ The unexpected return of Jesus is inevitable.

6. How might the recipients of Paul's words be feeling about the sudden, unavoidable destruction that Paul has illustrated with thievery and childbirth?

   What does Paul remind the Thessalonian Christians of in **5:4** that would ease any fears and worries?

7. Paul just told them what they are not. What does he proclaim their identity to be in **5:5**?

"Half of earth's gorgeousness lies hidden in the glimpsed city it longs to become. For all its rooted loveliness, the world has no continuing city here; it is an outlandish place, a foreign home, a session in via to a better version of itself—and it is our glory to see it so and thirst until Jerusalem comes home at last."

Robert Farrar Capon, *The Supper of the Lamb*

STUDY SKILL | TRACE A CONCEPT THROUGH SCRIPTURE

In your study of the scriptures you will come across words, phrases, and concepts that have been woven into the story of scripture. For Bible students to understand these themes more fully, we have to examine how that idea develops throughout the Bible. Using a Bible dictionary or even the cross references listed in a study Bible, you can look at and organize what's been said about a theme and then determine what about it is relevant to the passage or book you are studying.

Tracing a concept through the Bible helps us in a number of ways. For example, it takes words that feel overly familiar and transforms them into a masterpiece revealing new dimensions of meaning. You'll find tracing biblical themes can help make sense of confusing passages, bring together ideas you didn't realize were related, or connect the work of God with his character. This tool for considering the whole counsel of scripture will always open our minds to the fuller meaning of what we are studying and help us see God's work through history to bring about redemption.

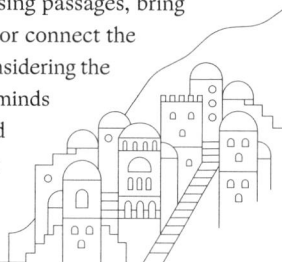

Let's put our study skill to work. We are going to look up verses dealing with the idea of "light" across three categories in which they are used throughout the Bible. You are going to be doing a lot of turning Bible pages in this section. You may want to use a Bible app or website like BibleGateway.com to look them up more efficiently. Either way the work will be worth it.

8. LIGHT AS AN ATTRIBUTE OF OUR HOLY GOD

Genesis 1:1–5	Who directs the light at creation?
2 Corinthians 4:6	Who directs the light of salvation?
1 Timothy 6:15–16	In what does God dwell?
John 8:12	What does Jesus call himself?
Revelation 21:23	Who illuminates the fully redeemed creation?

9. THE WORK OF LIGHT

Genesis 1:1–5	What does the light do to the original condition of the world?
Daniel 2:22	What does the light that dwells in God do?
Ecclesiastes 2:13	What is the advantage of light compared to?
2 Corinthians 4:6	What does the light reveal?

10. THE CHRISTIAN'S RELATIONSHIP TO THE LIGHT

Matthew 4:16	What do people who have experienced the light leave behind?
1 Peter 2:9	How are the people called into the light described?
	And what does that lead them to do?
Ephesians 5:8–9	What does the light create in people?
Matthew 5:14–16	What is one purpose of living a life of light now?

11. THE KINGDOM OF LIGHT

Colossians 1:9–13	To which kingdom do those who share in the inheritance of the light belong?
Luke 1:78–79	Has the kingdom of light begun to shine?
Revelation 22:3–5	When will the kingdom of the light be fully realized?

12. Now that you have done a quick look at the concept of light in the scriptures, let's apply it to the titles Paul gives to the Thessalonian Christians. How does each category from your study of "light" add a new dimension of understanding to the titles "children of the light" and "children of the day" (**5:5**)?

13. Paul doesn't stop at making their identity clear. He wants the Thessalonians to know that their identity has implications. Read **5:6–8** and contrast the ways in which those who belong to the night and those who belong to the day act in accordance with their identity.

Those Who Belong to the Night	Those Who Belong to the Day

14. According to **5:9–10**, how can the Thessalonians be sure that they belong to the day? Is this based on what they have done or what God has and will do for them?

15. Read **Ephesians 2:1–9** below. Take it slow, let the words weigh on you, and imagine the tone Paul would have intended for them to carry.

"And you were dead in your trespasses and sins in which you previously walked according to the ways of this world, according to the ruler of the power of the air, the spirit now working in the disobedient. We too all previously lived among them in our fleshly desires, carrying out the inclinations of our flesh and thoughts, and we were by nature children under wrath as the others were also. But God, who is rich in mercy, because of his great love that he had for us, made us alive with Christ even though we were dead in trespasses. You are saved by grace! He also raised us up with him and seated us with him in the heavens in Christ Jesus, so that in the coming ages he might display the immeasurable riches of his grace through his kindness to us in Christ Jesus. For you are saved by grace through faith, and this is not from yourselves; it is God's gift—not from works, so that no one can boast. For we are his workmanship, created in Christ Jesus for good works, which God prepared ahead of time for us to do."

Mark the following in these verses:
- Strike through everything Christians used to be, do, or belong to.
- Circle the attributes of God and the work of God.
- Draw a box around what Christians now are, do, and belong to.

16. Now, considering what we've read in **1 Thessalonians 5** and **Ephesians 2**, should Christians have anything to fear in the coming day of the Lord?

Paul ends this section in **verse 11** with the call to encourage one another with all that he has said in the previous ten verses. In what ways does this become a constant, powerful encouragement for those who belong to the day in their pursuit of a life that pleases God?

17. Let's recap Paul's main points from **5:1–11** before we move on to his closing words. Finish each point with the phrase that best characterizes what Paul wants the Thessalonians to know:

The timing of the day of the Lord (**5:1–4**)

_____ is of utmost importance and has been told to the Thessalonians.

_____ is unknowable, will be sudden and unexpected for those who aren't believers, and inevitable for all.

_____ is knowable if you track the puzzle pieces through scripture.

The way for Christians to be prepared for the day of the Lord is (**5:5–8**)

_____ to try and figure out the time the Lord will return.

_____ to joyfully expect Jesus Christ to return any time and live a life that pleases God as they wait.

_____ to forget that the day is coming and live their lives as they please.

Christians do not need to fear the day of the Lord because (**5:9–11**)

_____ God has not destined them for wrath because the same Jesus that came to save them is returning to spend eternity with them.

_____ they can be good enough to earn God's salvation in the end.

_____ God won't bring wrath.

"If the kingdom is good news, it surely isn't safe.
Because there is no square inch of our lives that
Jesus doesn't intend to rule."

Jen Pollock Michel, *Surprised by Paradox*

18. Paul finishes his letter with a series of rapid-fire exhortations. Some of these are general calls to holiness while others are specific to topics we have seen Paul cover in the letter. Read **5:12–22** and categorize as best you can what is general wisdom from an apostle and what is specific to the themes of Paul's letter to the Thessalonians.

General Wisdom	Specific to Themes of 1 Thessalonians

19. Why do you think God's people need both general wisdom and specific instruction for their circumstances? Do these two categories work together in any way?

20. Look at the list one more time. What attributes of God do you see reflected in this list? Use the attributes list in appendix C on page 154 to help with your answer.

21. Anyone who honestly assesses their own heart and actions will recognize that conforming to this list feels overwhelming.

Y	N	
		Do the Thessalonians have any hope of following these instructions in their own strength?
		According to **5:23**, do the Thessalonians have any hope of following these instructions in the strength of someone else?

If so, whose strength will enable them?

22. Look at **5:23–24** again. What degree of confidence can believers have that the God of peace can bring about holiness in their lives? How thoroughly will God complete this work?

23. What attribute of God does Paul credit for the certainty we have in his sanctifying work?

24. Which of the qualities does Paul demonstrate in **5:25–27**? Check all that apply:

____ humility   ____ care

____ partnership   ____ love

____ relationship   ____ authority

____ inclusion

25. What parting blessing does Paul conclude his letter with? Why do you think this a fitting end to all that Paul in partnership with Silas and Timothy has written?

WRAP-UP

26. Now that you have studied **1 Thessalonians 5:1–28**, write a short summary of the verses in your own words. Then identify how this text rehearses, explains, or reveals a part of the story of scripture or the entire story of scripture.

APPLY IT

THESE QUESTIONS ARE JUST TO GET YOU STARTED.
THIS SPACE IS OPEN FOR ANY REFLECTION AND APPLICATION.

PERSONAL

Humanity has always been fascinated with the question of what will happen at the end of the time. Do you feel more captivated with the "when" and "how" of the promised last day than the "why" and what it means for your life now? What lesson from chapter five can help you rightly value both?

Do you harbor any fear about the day of the Lord? How should Christ's future return inspire you toward hope and holiness now?

COMMUNAL

In what ways is your Christian community tempted to sleep instead of staying awake, alert, and active in your pursuit of holiness? What's one way you can help rouse a drowsy community? Is it coordinating a way for them to be involved in your neighborhood, reminding them of ways to encourage a suffering brother or sister, inviting someone more regularly into your home?

Paul refers to the community of believers as "brothers and sisters" more times in chapter 5 than any other chapter in 1 Thessalonians. Where does your Christian community excel when it comes to the familial love Paul describes? Take time to thank God for faithfully bringing about holiness in your community then text, call, or make a plan to thank a brother and sister for the way they are displaying familiar love.

UNIVERSAL

God's desire is for those who belong to the light to constantly grow. Has the church developed a reputation in society at large for wanting to add to its numbers? Where have you seen Christians do an impressive job of showing God's love to others and inviting them into his family in the way they talk, interact online, engage in politics, treat strangers, prioritize the vulnerable, or serve their community? What has been the result of this behavior?

What false messages of "peace and security" does society proclaim? What makes them so tempting to believe? What makes the gospel message and story of scripture more compelling?

07

Your Perseverance and Faith

2 THESSALONIANS 1:1–12

The second letter to the Thessalonians opens in a familiar way. By God's grace the Thessalonian church has grown in faith, love, and hope and Paul, Silas, and Timothy praise God for them. But their Christian character is not the only thing that has increased—opposition to the Thessalonian church is on the rise. Paul opens by addressing persecution, the first of three problematic situations facing the Thessalonian church. His encouragement reinforces the Thessalonians' standing in Christ and points them to the future day of vindication. God has promised a day when all wrongs will be righted. The Thessalonians may endure suffering for a moment, but they were bound for a day when the Lord himself would vindicate them.

GET FAMILIAR WITH THE WORDS ON THE PAGE. ————

2 THESSALONIANS 1:1–12

READ

Continue using the reading log in the back of your book to keep track of the number of times and ways you have read large sections or the entire book(s) of 1 and 2 Thessalonians.

OBSERVE

Write down some details you noticed during your reading and rereading making sure to include where you see the main themes addressed in this section. The list of things to look for is always in the introduction if you need a reminder. Make a goal to list at least twenty observations.

QUESTION

Reading for detail and listing your observations can jump start your intellect. Lean into your curiosity and write down questions or subjects you'd like to understand better in this week's text.

STUDY IT

WORK THROUGH THIS WEEK'S TEXT VERSE BY VERSE.

1. Compare and contrast the greeting in **1 Thessalonians 1:1** with the greeting in **2 Thessalonians 1:1–2**.

Similarities	Differences

2. Where does Paul locate the church of the Thessalonians in **1:1**? What do you think is the significance of this description?

3. Let's look at the bookends of **2 Thessalonians**. Fill in the blanks from **1:2** and **3:16**.

"Grace to you and _____ from God our Father and the Lord Jesus Christ." (**1:2**)

"May the Lord of_____ himself give you _____ _____ in _____ _____. The Lord be with all of you." (**3:16**)

4. Based on your initial reading of **2 Thessalonians**, can you see examples where peace emerges as a key feature of the book? Any in the first chapter specifically?

5. Paul's triad from **1 Thessalonians 1:3** makes an appearance again in **2 Thessalonians 1:3–4**. Fill in the chart with each attribute then note how the Thessalonians are progressing in each category. (Hint: The third characteristic is less straightforward than the first two. Remember to read for what "hope" is tied to in the initial description.)

Triad in **1 Thessalonians 1:3**	Paul's Analysis in **2 Thessalonians 1:3–4**
"Work produced by _____"	
"Labor motivated by _____"	
"Endurance inspired by _____ in our Lord Jesus Christ."	

6. In the copy of **1 Thessalonians 3:11–13** below, circle or highlight any part of Paul's prayer that God has begun to answer in **2 Thessalonians 1:3–4**.

"Now may our God and Father himself, and our Lord Jesus, direct our way to you. And may the Lord cause you to increase and overflow with love for one another and for everyone, just as we do for you. May he make your hearts blameless in holiness before our God and Father at the coming of our Lord Jesus with all his saints. Amen"

7. Paul bracketed his teaching with blessings and prayers for peace. In **1:3–6**, Paul introduces the first of three groups who are disrupting that peace. Which group does he address first and what topic does he cover in order to reassure the Thessalonian Christians.

Disrupter	Topic:
Idlers	Righteous Judgment
Persecutors	Right teaching
False Teachers	Righteous Living

8. Use your imagination to put yourself in the place of the Thessalonian believers suffering all kinds of persecution. What questions might you have for Paul, Silas, and Timothy about your situation and your faith?

Theology Primer

Most people are quick to affirm that evil seems to prosper. We hear of horrific acts far too frequently to believe otherwise—terrorists gruesomely murder strangers, child abusers pummel the unprotected, rapists ravage their victims and heap shame on them, and entire people groups are systematically executed for years before anyone seems to notice. Every tragedy causes our hearts to cry out with the psalmist: "How long will the wicked celebrate?" (Psalm 94:3). When presented with clear wrongs we want them righted. Even though we celebrate the idea of justice generally, we have trouble celebrating justice as an attribute of God. To see God's justice rightly and celebrate it like the authors of the Bible, we need to understand its foundations.

God's justice doesn't spring from anger or cruelty. The basis for God's justice is his love. Each fiber of the human heart that glows red with anger over the injustices of the world is fueled by love for the victimized. The same goes for God, except every victim carries his image. He witnesses every detail of every suffering. Every evil deed opposes his kingdom. And he holds the power to punish the wickedness that plagues the world. If the human heart burns with anger because of love, the heart of God is a love-fueled incinerator and he is morally bound to exercise his wrath.

God's just judgment against wickedness is integral to his plan to redeem all of creation. Since sin entered the world humanity has proven incapable of rejecting evil and instituting God's righteous kingdom. The story of scripture shows over and again that God must be the one to act in power to right the wrongs of the world. But if God is to righteously judge those who oppose his kingdom, every person should receive God's condemnation. All of us have acted unjustly and all of us deserve the wrath of God (Romans 3:23). If God decided to simply look the other way to include us in his perfect kingdom, he would no longer be just. For humanity to be included in God's redeemed kingdom, God himself must purify his people without denying his justice.

God's plan and desire has always been that the people he created would reign with him in his kingdom. The same love that fuels God's justice fuels his divine plan to save humanity from his wrath, which comes to fruition in the life, death, resurrection, and ascension of Jesus Christ. God sent his Son to save the world that condemned itself by its own sin. Jesus Christ, the Son of God, lived a perfect life of righteousness, died the death that God's justice requires, and rose from the dead proving his power over all wickedness. Because of Jesus' life and work, God offers humanity a secure place in his kingdom because his justice has been executed and his wrath against the unjust has been absorbed by Jesus (1 John 1:9). The only requirement to rest in God's grace instead of expecting his wrath is to trust in the person and work of Jesus Christ as salvation.

God is constantly drawing history toward its climax—the redemption of all things. He promises that on the day Jesus Christ returns all creation will be remade, all God's people will have their tears wiped away, death dies, and pain is banished (Revelation 21:4). God is working to right what is wrong. It is the love-fueled justice of God that brings this glorious vindication about. And it is his love-fueled offer to all of humanity to trust in Jesus Christ that allows people to be redeemed instead of condemned. The great scandal of God's justice is not that all deserve his wrath, but that some do not experience it. It is both somber and celebratory that God's love-fueled justice rights the world.

"God's good government ensures that justice will ultimately prevail in all things. It answers to no higher government, and it suffers no corruption."

Jen Wilkin, *In His Image: 10 Ways God Calls Us to Reflect His Character*

9. Which of the following do you think is the "evidence" Paul references in **1:5** of God's righteous judgment in favor of the Thessalonians?

_____ The suffering that has come their way

_____ Their response of faith, love, and endurance during the suffering

_____ Both the suffering and the Thessalonians' response to it

10. The Bible doesn't pretend suffering won't come. In fact, Paul has already reminded the Thessalonians in his first letter that persecution is likely. Read the following verses and note what you learn about the nature of suffering and what it develops in Christians:

Mark 8:34–35

Philippians 1:27–29

1 Peter 5:10

James 1:2–4

11. Considering the above verses as well as what we learned in **1 Thessalonians**. Which of the following do you think Paul is communicating in **1:5** when he says the Thessalonians will be "counted" worthy of God's kingdom?

_____ The Thessalonian' suffering and response qualifies them for the kingdom of God.

_____ God deems Christians worthy for his kingdom and ultimately uses their suffering for their good as a means to prepare them for his kingdom.

12. Paul's encouragement to the Thessalonian believers enduring persecution is twofold. In the chart, list what Paul says in **1:5–7** about the fate of the Thessalonians and that of their persecutors.

Future of the Thessalonian Christians	Future of Their Persecutors

FOLLOW THE LOGIC

13. It seems Paul knows his brothers and sisters in Thessalonica will likely have some questions. Let's follow Paul's line of logic in **verses 7–9** and see how he preemptively answers those:

When will the vindication of God and his people come?

"This will take place at the_____ of the _____ _____ from _____ with his powerful angels" (**v. 7b**).

Who all will experience God's punishment when he vindicates his people?

"When he takes vengeance with flaming fire on those who _____ _____ _____ and on those who _____ _____ the _____ of our Lord Jesus." (**v. 8**).

What will the punishment be like?

"They will pay the penalty of _____ _____from the _____ _____ and from his glorious _____" (**v. 9**).

14. Let's focus on the details in **verses 6–7**.

   Yes | No Does Paul seem certain that Jesus will return again?

   Yes | No Does Paul seem certain that Jesus will set the world right?

   Yes | No Will setting the world right bring peace for persecuted Christians?

15. Now let's look closer at **verses 8–9**.

What two things did the group who will receive punishment reject during their life?	1._____ 2._____
What two things does eternal destruction consist of for the group who will receive punishment experience?	1._____ 2._____

16. Look back at **1 Thessalonians 4:17**. What is the ultimate eternal outcome for all Christians?

17. How would you characterize the relationship between what those receiving punishment choose in this life and what they will receive in the next?

Now think about Christians. How would you characterize the relationship between what they choose in this life and what they will receive in the next?

18. Having looked closely at Paul's explanation of the fate of the wicked, does it change how you think or feel about the actions of God to right the world on the day of the Lord?

"We have all rejected God and deserve his rejection in return. The choice we have is this: to face hell by ourselves or to hide ourselves in Christ."

Rebecca McLaughlin, *Confronting Christianity: 12 Hard Questions for the World's Largest Religion*

We said in our study of 1 Thessalonians 5 that our tendency when we study the Lord's return is to get caught up in trying to decipher God's methodology. Let's acknowledge the parameters of what Paul is and isn't telling us in these verses.

19. Does **1:6–9** give us exact details on exactly how God's punishment is going to be carried out? What general premise does Paul communicate about the punishment?

Is Paul's purpose in these verses to satisfy our curiosity about God's judgment and hell in particular? Why does he bring up the righteous judgment of God?

20. Jesus spoke many times about the glory of eternal life (heaven) and the tragedy of eternal punishment (hell) during his ministry (see **Matthew 7:13–23; 8:10–13; 25:31–36**), but he also talked about the purpose of his gospel message—he was bringing the kingdom of God. In the Gospel of John, Jesus explains why God sent his Son into the world to a Jewish religious ruler named Nicodemus. Read **John 3:16–18**. This may be a very familiar set of verses to you. If so, remind yourself to read slowly and for detail.

*"For God loved the world in this way: He gave his one and only Son, so that everyone who believes in him will not perish but have eternal life. For God did not send his Son into the world to condemn the world, but to save the world through him. Anyone who believes in him is not condemned, but anyone who does not believe is already condemned, because he has not believed in the name of the one and only Son of God." –***John 3:16–18**

Now, mark the following things in these verses:
- Circle the attributes and actions of God in this text
- Strike through what God did not send his Son to accomplish
- Draw a box around what God did send his Son to accomplish
- Highlight how a person avoids condemnation

21. God's heart to save the world rather than condemn it shows up long before Jesus is born—it's evident from the earliest pages of the Bible. Look up the following verses and note what you learn about God and his desire for humanity.

Genesis 3:15	What does God plan to do to humanity's greatest enemy?
Exodus 34:5–6	What does God abound in?
	At what pace does God's anger escalate?
Ezekiel 18:32	What doesn't God find pleasure in?
	What does God find pleasure in?
1 Timothy 2:1–4	What does Paul urge Christians to do?
	What is God's desire?

22. The name of Jesus may be disparaged by those who reject God in this life, but what great reversal will happen when Jesus returns according to **1:10**?

23. Read **1:11**. How does Paul connect the future promise of glorification for Jesus and his people at his return with the present lives of the Thessalonians?

24. What is the ultimate goal Paul prays for in **1:12**?

25. Paul's prayer is reminiscent of the prayer Jesus prays for all believers. Look up **John 17:1–26**. What similarities do you see between the two prayers? How do Jesus's words expand your understanding of Paul's prayer?

26. How do Paul's words in this first chapter encourage and strengthen the Thessalonians facing opposition from persecutors?

WRAP-UP

27. Now that you have studied **2 Thessalonians 1:1–12**, write a short summary of the verses in your own words. Then identify how this text rehearses, explains, or reveals a part of the story of scripture or the entire story of scripture.

APPLY IT

PERSONAL

Consider how God has begun to answer some of the prayers you have prayed. How does keeping a record of God's faithfulness encourage you toward hope?

The thought of Jesus returning in judgment and sending people to hell makes most of us uncomfortable. How should that feeling simultaneously move us to hope and encouragement and drive us toward active gospel proclamation among those who do not believe?

COMMUNAL

Amidst persecution and suffering, Paul noticed in the Thessalonian church a growing love for one another. Is your love for your brothers and sisters in Christ growing? What steps can you take to increase your love for your Christian family at all times?

Paul assured the Thessalonian church that they were defined by their place in God's family through the work of Christ—not by their difficult circumstances. How does our perspective on suffering change knowing that God works on our behalf and uses his church in the midst of suffering to represent his kingdom to the world?

UNIVERSAL

The story of scripture is marked by rejection of God and rebellion against his kingdom. Do most people believe the narrative of rebellion or a narrative that people are generally good? Why is understanding our nature of rebellion important to the spread of the gospel message?

We saw that God does not delight in the destruction of the wicked, but in order for God to right the world and fully institute his perfect kingdom he must judge the wicked and those who oppose his kingdom ways. By this standard, every one should expect condemnation. Think back to what you read in John 3 and write out how you might explain to someone how Jesus is the bridge between God's just salvation and his just condemnation.

08

Stand Firm & Hold Fast

2 THESSALONIANS 2:1–17

Having bolstered the hope and fortitude of the Thessalonians in the face of persecution, Paul and his companions move on to the second issue creating opposition. Some people were teaching a message that contradicted the apostle. The false teaching threatened to infiltrate the Thessalonians and sow chaos and confusion among the fledgling church. Paul brings clarity and calms the Thessalonians by grounding them in what is true. By focusing on the truth they would not be shaken by falsehood.

GET FAMILIAR WITH THE WORDS ON THE PAGE.

2 THESSALONIANS 2:1–17

READ

Continue using the reading log in the back of your book to keep track of the number of times and ways you have read large sections or the entire book(s) of 1 and 2 Thessalonians.

OBSERVE

Write down some details you noticed during your reading and rereading making sure to include where you see the main themes addressed in this section. Remember, the goal is at least twenty observations.

QUESTION

Indulge your curiosity and write down your questions about the Bible text.

STUDY IT

1. In **2:1–4**, Paul introduces the second group disrupting the peace. Which group does he address and what topic does he cover in order to bring clarity to the Thessalonian Christians?

Disrupter	Topic:
Idlers	Righteous Judgment
Persecutors	Right teaching
False Teachers	Righteous Living

2. Look at **2:1**. What subject matter were the false teachers distorting?

3. Look up **2:2** in a different translation of your choice to add to your understanding of the people's reaction. What response to false teaching does Paul ask the Thessalonians to actively avoid? How effective could false teachers be at disrupting the peace?

4. Based on Paul's instruction in **2:2**, what tactics do the false teachers seem to implement?

5. According to **2:2**, the false teaching the Thessalonian were in danger of believing was:

_____ The day of the Lord had already arrived

_____ Paul wasn't an apostle

_____ Jesus wasn't the Messiah

6. What does **2:3** explain the Thessalonians are in danger of if they don't heed Paul's instruction about keeping their composure?

7. Look up **2 Peter 2:1–3**. How does Peter characterize the instruction of false teachers? Does Peter take their presence and power among God's people as seriously as Paul in **2 Thessalonians**?

The false teachers worked to sell the Thessalonians on a false story about the end times. To combat their lies and reassure the Thessalonians, Paul reminds them of the true story of what is happening, what will happen before Jesus returns, and what will take place at his return. But before we examine the details we need to acknowledge our limits. Verse 5 makes it clear that the Thessalonians received teaching from Paul in person on this topic that he does not reiterate in his letters. Twenty centuries later we do not share the same information with Paul's original audience. But our lack of knowledge surrounding the details in this story shouldn't induce worry or anxiety, God has purposely crafted his Word for our benefit knowing we wouldn't know all that Paul had previously taught the Thessalonians. Recognizing these God-ordained gaps in our knowledge should amplify our humility, not our speculation. We can approach this text confident that what we do know from 2 Thessalonians provides the information we need to grow in understanding and holiness. In our study we will resist frenzied attempts to solve a puzzle and instead cultivate confidence in God's Word and prepare ourselves to live as those who belong to the day.

8. See the list of characters involved in the story of the end times. Two of them are new to the books of **1 and 2 Thessalonians**. List what you learn in **2:3–12** about the actions and character of the lawless one and what you learn about the role of the restrainer.

Cast of Characters:

God   The Lord Jesus   Satan   Those who are perishing

The Restrainer   The Lawless One

The Restrainer	**The Lawless One**
Role	Actions & Character

9. As Paul retells this story to the Thessalonians, he moves back and forth in time while revealing the chronological order of events. The story told in **2:3–10** unfolds in three stages. Place each event from the list in its correct chronological stage.

Events:		
The lawless one is revealed	**Current Time of Restraint**	(2:7a)
Mystery of lawlessness is at work		(2:6a)
The Lord Jesus returns	**Future Time of Rebellion**	(2:7b)
The restrainer is holding back the full force of lawlessness		(2:3b; 8a)
The lawless one is destroyed by the breath of the Lord Jesus		(2:9–10)
All kinds of false miracles, signs, and wonders done by the power of Satan deceive those who are perishing		(2:3a)
The apostasy (a great rebellion) breaks out	**Ultimate Day of Retribution**	(2:8c)
The removal of the restrainer of lawlessness		(2:8b)

"Rebellion occurs, not because individuals make a conscious decision to rebel against God, even though they know that only God is God and that they are God's creatures. They rebel because they are deluded into believing that they have no need of God or that they already know God's mind."

Beverly Roberts Gaventa, *First and Second Thessalonians*

10. Trying to identify the specific events Paul outlines as well as the identities of the lawless one and the restrainer have captivated the minds of people throughout history. Answer the following questions about what Paul communicates regarding the plans and purposes of God in these verses.

T	F	
		Paul's audience seems to know the identity of the restrainer.
		Paul clearly states who or what each character is for future readers to know their identities.
		Paul's teaching here contradicts what he taught about the sudden return of Jesus in 1 Thessalonians 4.
		The details we get confirm that God works through history to overcome evil and right the world.

11. Having assessed the characters and the plot, let's look at some of the details we are given about the lawless one.

The lawless one is in league with (**2:9**): _____

The lawless one claims to be (**2:4**): _____

The lawless one is a master of wicked (**2:10**) :

_____

12. These verses present the lawless one as a fierce, terror-inducing enemy who is unafraid to take on God. What would you expect it to take to vanquish that kind of enemy? What does Paul tell us it will actually take for the Lord Jesus to vanquish the lawless one?

13. Look up the following verses and note what you learn about the power of the breath of God.

Job 4:9

Psalm 33:6

Isaiah 11:4

14. Do the verses above and Paul's description of what will happen when Jesus returns leave any room for believing that God will be defeated?

15. Paul gives even further explanation in **2:10–12**. Which group does Paul address in these verses?

16. In **verse 11** Paul says that God sends a delusion to those who are perishing. What is your first reaction to that statement?

FOLLOW THE LOGIC

17. The idea that God sends a delusion that brings about judgment likely sets off our internal alarm. We determined in our study of **2 Thessalonians 1** that God does not delight in anyone's destruction. Similar to the timeline of end events, Paul moves back and forth in time in his explanation. Let's untangle the logic in **2:10** and **2:12** to better understand Paul's statement.

Who will be deceived by the lawless one?

"And with every wicked deception among _____ who_____

_____" (**v. 10a**).

Why are some people already perishing?

"They perish _____ they did _____ _____ the _____

of the _____" (**v. 10b**).

What did they love instead of the truth?

"Those who did not believe the truth but _____ in

_____" (**v. 12b**).

What would have happened if they had chosen to love the truth?

"And so _____ _____" (**v. 10c**).

STUDY SKILL | REPLACE PRONOUNS

Often a verse uses a pronoun—he, she, we, that, this, that, it, etc.—to reference a previously mentioned or forthcoming person, group, place, thing, or idea. At times, we may replace the pronoun with the wrong specific noun or miss the intended meaning by misunderstanding what the author says. In order to provide clarity and increase your understanding of a verse, you should read the verse in context and trace the pronouns to what they reference in order to specify which he, she, we, that, this, that, or it the author has in view.

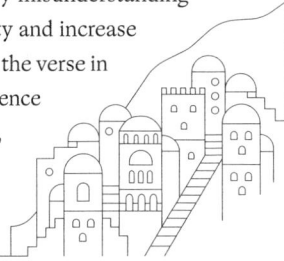

18. Now that we understand the context that sets up Paul's alarming statement, let's trace the pronouns to provide further clarify. Put a check mark next to the correct replacement for each pronoun.

For **this** reason

_____ Because those who are perishing have chosen to delight in unrighteousness and refuse to believe or love the truth
_____ Because God wants to punish someone
_____ Because those who are perishing had no choice

God sends **them**

_____ A randomly chosen group of people
_____ Those God hates
_____ Those who rejected God

So that **they** will believe the lie

_____ Those who already refused the truth
_____ Those who previously knew the truth
_____ A randomly chosen group of people

19. Now, rewrite **2:11** using the statements you chose above in place of the pronouns.

20. Paul expands on the progression we see in **2 Thessalonians 2:10–12** in his letter to the church in Rome.

> *"And because they did not think it worthwhile to acknowledge God, God delivered them over to a corrupt mind so that they do what is not right. They are filled with all unrighteousness, evil, greed, and wickedness. They are full of envy, murder, quarrels, deceit, and malice. They are gossips, slanderers, God-haters, arrogant, proud, boastful, inventors of evil, disobedient to parents, senseless, untrustworthy, unloving, and unmerciful. Although they know God's just sentence—that those who practice such things deserve to die—they not only do them, but even applaud others who practice them."* –**Romans 1:28–32**

Mark the following things in these verses:
- Circle what this group chose to believe about God
- Underline God's response to their choice
- Draw a box around the consequences of their choice

> "Loyalty to apostolic teaching, now permanently enshrined in the New Testament, is still the test of truth and the shield against error."
>
> John R. W. Stott, *The Bible Speaks Today: The Message of 1 & 2 Thessalonians*

21. Based on **2:13**, does Paul believe the Thessalonians will be deceived by the false teachers and choose the lie over the truth? What is Paul's response to the Thessalonians' faith?

22. Look closely at what Paul outlines in **verses 13–14**. List the reasons Paul has confidence that the Thessalonians will make it through persecution and false teaching to the glory of Jesus Christ.

23. What are the first two words of **2:15**?

   "_____ _____, brothers and sisters, stand firm and hold to the traditions you were taught, whether by what we said or what we wrote."

24. In light of his confidence that God has saved the Thessalonians and is faithful to bring them into the promised glory, Paul calls them in **verse 15** to do two things. List them here.

   1) _____

   2) _____

25. With false teachers spreading lies around them, where has Paul just told the Thessalonians to train their focus?

   _____ On understanding the false teaching

   _____ On relaxing and not worrying about what is taught

   _____ On clinging to the Word of God given to them by the apostles

26. Paul ends this chapter with a prayer addressed to both "our Lord Jesus Christ" and "God our Father" that describes the gifts they give to believers. What are those gifts? Are the gifts mentioned things the Thessalonians experience as they wait for Jesus to return or at Jesus's return?

27. Look up **James 1:16–18**. What can children of the day expect from God?

28. What evidence of God's encouragement and hope does Paul pray in **2:17** to see in the Thessalonians?

29. Think back over all Paul has said. How have his words instilled confidence in a Christian community shaken and scared by false teachers?

WRAP-UP

30. Now that you have studied **2 Thessalonians 2:1–17**, write a short summary of the verses in your own words. Then identify how this text rehearses, explains, or reveals a part of the story of scripture or the entire story of scripture.

THESE QUESTIONS ARE JUST TO GET YOU STARTED.
THIS SPACE IS OPEN FOR ANY REFLECTION AND APPLICATION.

APPLY IT

PERSONAL

Paul clearly lays out the power of the Word of God to protect his people from false teaching. Do you tend to think of your time in God's Word as a means of protection for your faith? If not, how might this perspective change your approach to your time in the scriptures?

Do you believe that you could fall prey to false teaching? Why is it important to recognize your vulnerability? Take time to write out a prayer asking God to help you avoid deception and stand firm in his Word.

COMMUNAL

When the Thessalonians bring up false teaching, Paul doesn't say, "Don't be silly." He says, "Take the Word of God seriously." Then he reminds them of what is true. What are we in danger of when we don't take seriously our responsibility to help one another discern truth from lies? What are some practical ways you could begin to more fully embrace this responsibility in your Christian community?

Every group of Christians is prone to over or under emphasize the Bible's end times teachings. Where does your church or close group of Christian friends and family fall on that spectrum? How might you need to change your perspective so that the Bible's end times teachings drive you toward the goal of increasing your holiness?

UNIVERSAL

God's victory against his enemies is sure and certain and he wants to share his victory with his people. How would you tell the story of God's ultimate victory to someone who feels like a victim of injustice? What about to someone who feels mostly like a perpetrator of injustice?

What are some of the attractive false teachings offered to humanity by those who reject God? Which are you tempted to believe? What would change in your world if you regularly reminded yourself of God's true enemies and his ultimate victory?

09

Peace Always in Every Way

2 THESSALONIANS 3:1–18

At first glance, Paul's final topic feels like a hard right turn. From judgment, vindication, and the vanquishing of God's enemies we turn the page to find Paul redirecting his attention to the here and now. He begins by focusing on how the church grows wider to include more people and then calls the church to grow deeper in the faith. Some Thessalonian believers were resisting maturity rejecting the teaching of the apostle. These idle believers had put an undue burden on their brothers and sisters and made themselves a threat to the peace in the Thessalonian church. In word and deed Paul, Silas, and Timothy had taught the Thessalonians how to live as Christians as they awaited Jesus's return. Paul's final words remind the Thessalonian church that those who belong to the day long for the salvation of many and work for the sanctification of the saved.

GET FAMILIAR WITH THE WORDS ON THE PAGE. ————————

2 THESSALONIANS 3:1–18

READ

Continue using the reading log in the back of your book to keep track of the number of times and ways you have read large sections or the entire book(s) of 1 and 2 Thessalonians.

OBSERVE

Write down some details you noticed during your reading and rereading making sure to include where you see the main themes addressed in this section. The list of things to look for is always in the introduction if you need a reminder. Make a goal to list at least twenty observations.

QUESTION

Reading for detail and listing your observations can jump start your intellect. Lean into your curiosity and write down questions or subjects you'd like to understand better in this week's text.

STUDY IT

WORK THROUGH THIS WEEK'S TEXT VERSE BY VERSE.

1. **Chapter 3** opens with a prayer and at this point, we shouldn't be surprised. Prayer has marked every chapter of **1 and 2 Thessalonians** except for one. Look back through the many times we have seen Paul pray or mention prayer and write down what he teaches or models in each instance.

	Paul's Teaching and Example
1 Thess. 1:2–3	
1 Thess. 2:13	
1 Thess. 3:9–10	
1 Thess. 3:11–13	
1 Thess. 5:17	
1 Thess. 5:23–24	
1 Thess. 5:25	
2 Thess. 1:3	
2 Thess. 1:11–12	
2 Thess. 2:13	
2 Thess. 2:16–17	
2 Thess. 3:1–2	
2 Thess. 3:5	
2 Thess. 3:16	

2. In **Philippians 4:6** Paul writes, "Don't worry about anything, but in everything, through prayer and petition with thanksgiving, present your requests to God." How has Paul put his own teaching about prayer into practice in **1 and 2 Thessalonians**?

3. Now look specifically at Paul's prayer in **3:1–2** and note the details.

Who does Paul request prayer from?	_____
Who does Paul request prayer for?	_____
What two things does Paul request prayer for?	1. _____ 2. _____

4. Paul wanted the "word of the Lord" to grow. In **3:1–5** he beckons the Thessalonians to partner with him, Silas, and Timothy so that it would grow in what way:

_____ **Breadth**—bringing new people into the kingdom of God

_____ **Depth**— bringing the lives of Christians into fuller alignment with the kingdom of God

5. Paul just spent two chapters emphasizing the reality of God's wrath toward those who reject him. How do **verses 1–2** reinforce the truth that God sent his Son to save the world rather than condemn it?

6. Based on **3:1–2**, what does Paul seem to believe about the role of prayer in the spread of the word of the Lord?

7. Read **verses 3–5**. What should bolster the Thessalonians' confidence to approach God with their requests?

"What a privilege it is to build our relationship with God through prayer—to honestly share our hearts with the One who perplexes us, saves our souls, created the universe with a word, and is the author and finisher of our faith."

Mary DeMuth, *Pray Every Day: 90 Days of Prayer from God's Word*

8. Starting in **3:6**, Paul beckons the Thessalonians to obey what he, Silas, and Timothy have taught them so that the word of the Lord would grow in what way:

_____ **Breadth**—bringing new people into the kingdom of God

_____ **Depth**— bringing the lives of Christians into fuller alignment with the kingdom of God

9. In **3:6**, Paul introduces the third group disrupting the peace. Which group does he address and what topic does he cover in order to sanctify the Thessalonian church?

Disrupter	Topic:
Idlers	Righteous Judgment
Persecutors	Right teaching
False Teachers	Righteous Living

10. Paul has addressed this group once before. Reread his admonition in **1 Thessalonians 4:9–12**? Have the idle heeded Paul's first instruction? How has Paul's tone changed?

11. Apparently, Paul knew Christians may be tempted to idleness. Based on **3:7–9**, what did Paul and his companions do in order to encourage the Thessalonians to combat that temptation?

12. Look ahead to **3:11**. How does Paul describe the idle? Write the title Paul gives them in the blank and then choose which definition best characterizes the people Paul has in mind.

"They are not busy but

_____ *"* (**v. 11b**).

_____ They are unable to work so they rely on the generosity of others and keep themselves busy working for the good of the community in whatever way they can.

_____ They meddle in the affairs of others and choose to exploit the generosity of others instead of working to support themselves.

_____ They are more worried about the behavior of other people than they are their own behavior.

13. We can deduce how the idle behaved based on how Paul described the example of he and his companions to the Thessalonians in **3:7–8**. Complete each phrase defining Paul and his companions' behavior, then write what it implies about the idle Thessalonians.

Paul's Behavior

Paul and his companions were not (**v.7b**):

And they did not (**v. 8a**):

Instead they (**v. 8b**):

So they would not be (**v. 8c**):

What it Implies

He is admonishing those who are:

Who did:

And refused to:

And therefore become a:

14. Paul prayed in **2 Thessalonians 1:11–12**:

   "In view of this, we always pray for you that our God will make you worthy of his calling, and by his power fulfill your every desire to do good and your work produced by faith, so that the name of our Lord Jesus will be glorified by you, and you by him, according to the grace of our God and the Lord Jesus Christ."

Underline or highlight the aspects of Paul's prayer that the idle Thessalonians are failing to live up to. Then use the chart to describe how their failure is likely affecting their gospel witness and their Christian relationships.

Effects on Their Gospel Witness	Effects on their Christian Relationships

15. Paul lays out how he expects the faithful Thessalonians to discipline the idle among them. According to **3:6**, how seriously does he expect the faithful Thessalonians to take his instructions?

16. Paul's instructions for discipline are not to be applied indiscriminately. Look closely at **3:6–15** and then circle the option in each pair that best characterizes Paul's instructions on discipline.

Who does Paul say should be disciplined for their idleness?

Those whose offense is:

Deliberate	OR	Accidental
A one time event		Persistent
Offensive to any person		Disobedient to the apostles' teaching

How did Paul instruct the discipline to be carried out?

The discipline should be:

Private	OR	Social in nature
A relief of the burden from the community		A requirement for the community to support the idle
Implemented by the whole Christian community		Implemented by the church leadership

What was the purpose of this discipline?

The goal of the discipline is:

Shame that brings repentance	OR	Shame that brings humiliation
Making the offender an enemy		Warning the offender in love as family
Restoration to the Christian community		Permanent excommunication

17. In **3:10** Paul reiterates what he already taught the Thessalonians about work. Look up **Genesis 3:19**. What do God's proclamation and Paul's teaching have in common?

18. Look up the following verses and note what you learn about how the family of God is to care for one another and those in need.

Matthew 25:34–40

Acts 4:32–35

1 Peter 4:9–10

19. What about these examples and instructions differs from Paul's declaration: "If anyone isn't willing to work, he should not eat?" Do these instructions contradict or complement one another?

"Our faith is proved genuine by our obedience—
expressed in love for the God who rescued us
from sin and death and in love for others."

Carmen Joy Imes, *Bearing God's Name: Why Sinai Still Matters*

20. In **3:13** Paul urges the faithful Thessalonians to keep up the good work saying, "But as for you, brothers and sisters, do not grow weary in doing good." What about idleness in the Christian community exhausts the faithful? What might their exhaustion lead to?

21. Paul says something similar to the Galatians. Read **Galatians 6:7–10** below. How does it expand your understanding of Paul's instruction not to grow weary in doing good?

    "Don't be deceived: God is not mocked. For whatever a person sows he will also reap, because the one who sows to his flesh will reap destruction from the flesh, but the one who sows to the Spirit will reap eternal life from the Spirit. Let us not get tired of doing good, for we will reap at the proper time if we don't give up. Therefore, as we have opportunity, let us work for the good of all, especially for those who belong to the household of faith."

22. Having addressed the three groups and the issues threatening the peace God has for his people, Paul writes his final greeting. Write out his final prayer in **3:16**.

23. What does Paul expect the Thessalonians to receive from the Lord despite the reality of persecution, the threat of false teaching, and the burden of the disobedient in the church? Look up **John 14:27**. How does this verse add weight to Paul's final prayer for the Thessalonians?

24. Why is it important that Paul authenticates this message in **3:17**?

25. What parting blessing does Paul use to conclude his letter? How is it a fitting end to the encouragement, hope, and instruction Paul, Silas, and Timothy have just poured out to people who belong to the day?

WRAP-UP

26. Now that you have studied **2 Thessalonians 3:1–18**, write a short summary of the verses in your own words. Then identify how this text rehearses, explains, or reveals a part of the story of scripture or the entire story of scripture.

APPLY IT

PERSONAL

The idle among the Thessalonians had heard Paul's instructions on how to live and chose to reject them. What teaching from the Word of God are you tempted to reject? What about Paul's instructions to the idle can help you realign your life with God's stated ways?

Prayer saturates the pages of 1 and 2 Thessalonians. Have you cultivated a practice of prayer? If so, how did you nurture that habit? If not, what is one activity you do everyday you can partner with prayer to help you cultivate the habit of praying everyday?

COMMUNAL

Paul's teaching on how to discipline those who reject the apostles' teaching assumes the Christian community shares their lives and their resources with one another. Is your church or faith community sharing life in a way that exposes sin and allows for Paul's instructions to be effective? If not, what is one step you can take to share your life more with your Christian brothers and sisters?

Paul's prayers demonstrate a longing for the spiritual growth of his brothers and sisters in Christ. Are you concerned for the spiritual life of your brothers and sisters? Make a list of those close to you and write a specific attribute of God you long to see grow in them. Pray to that end every day this week.

UNIVERSAL

When part of the Christian community actively rejects any teaching of God's Word it hinders the proclamation of the gospel. Why does your personal holiness matter to your neighborhood, your city, your workplace, your country, and the world at large?

Paul ends his letter with an effusive prayer for peace. When you look at the world around you do you see peace? Take a minute to think about the implications of God bringing peace, then emulate Paul and write a specific prayer for peace in the world around you.

10

Conclusion

You did it! Starting a Bible study is commendable, but finishing it deserves no small congratulations. Regardless of whether or not working through these pages was easy or a struggle, you have studied every verse of 1 and 2 Thessalonians. As you worked your way through the questions, you did more than pull these books apart—you put them back together to understand their power, their message, and their place in the story of scripture. To finish your study, reflect on these books as a whole and spend time considering how God has and will continue to use them to cultivate your faith.

GET FAMILIAR WITH THE WORDS ON THE PAGE. ————————————

KNOW IT

READ

For the final time of your study, read through both 1 and 2 Thessalonians and record your reading of the books in your reading log.

OBSERVE

Let's do something different for your final set of observations. Note which verses have taken on a new meaning for you, which have expanded your understanding about a particular attribute of God, which brought clarity to an area where you were confused, and which continue to come back to mind after you studied them.

QUESTION

Reading for detail and listing your observations can jump start your intellect. Lean into your curiosity and write down questions or subjects you'd like to understand better in this week's text.

STUDY IT

1. In our introduction to this study, we reminded ourselves that the Bible is telling one story of God bringing redemption to a sin wrecked world. From what we've learned in **1 and 2 Thessalonians**, how important was it to Paul that Christians knew the story of the scriptures? Why?

2. What would be missing in our study of the story of the Bible if **1 and 2 Thessalonians** were absent?

3. List the major themes we discussed in the introduction and that you've been noting in your weekly reading. What have you learned about each theme?

4. Major themes in any book of the Bible are most likely themes present in the larger story of scripture. Think about the themes once more, but this time ask how you see them play out or develop through God's story of bringing redemption to a evil-wrecked world.

5. Now that you have studied both **1 and 2 Thessalonians**, write a short summary of these books in your own words.

In what ways has the Holy Spirit shown you the truth that if you proclaim Jesus as Lord and believe in your heart that God raised him from the dead that you are surely a child of light who belongs to the day?

Have Paul's words accomplished in you what he hoped to accomplish in the Thessalonians—encouragement, hope, assurance, understanding, holiness, and a reliance on God?

Paul invited each Christian into their rightful place in the story of scriptures. Has your perspective changed or expanded in terms of how your story is part of God's story? Where do you want this change to have the greatest impact on your daily life?

What have you learned about God through your study of **1 and 2 Thessalonians** that makes you want to please him more?

ENDNOTES

PART TWO

K., Gupta Nijay. *1-2 Thessalonians A New Covenant Commentary.* Cambridge: Lutteworth Press, 2017, page 39.

Stott, John R. W. T*he Message of 1 & 2 Thessalonians.* Downers Grove, IL, U.S.A.: InterVarsity Press, 1994, page 35.

PART THREE

McLaughlin, Rebecca. Confronting Christianity: *12 Hard Questions for the Worlds Largest Religion.* Wheaton: Crossway, 2019, page 156.

Gaventa, Beverly Roberts. *First and Second Thessalonians.* Louisville, KY: Westminster John Knox Press, 2012, page 35.

PART FOUR

Wright, N. T. *Paul for Everyone: Galatians and Thessalonians.* Louisville, KY: Westminster John Knox Press, 2004, page 107.

K., Gupta Nijay. *1-2 Thessalonians A New Covenant Commentary.* Cambridge: Lutterworth Press, 2017, page 71.

PART FIVE

Michel, Jen Pollock. *Surprised by Paradox: The Promise of and in an Either-or World.* Downers Grove: InterVarsity Press, 2019, page 139.

Stott, John R. W. T*he Message of 1 & 2 Thessalonians.* Downers Grove, IL, U.S.A.: InterVarsity Press, 1994, page 85.

PART SIX

Capon, Robert Farrar. *The Supper of the Lamb: A Culinary Reflection.* New York: Modern Library, 2002, page 189.

Michel, Jen Pollock. *Surprised by Paradox: The Promise of and in an Either-or World.* Downers Grove: InterVarsity Press, 2019, page 68.

PART SEVEN

Wilkin, Jen. *In His Image: 10 Ways God Calls Us to Reflect His Character.* Wheaton, IL: Crossway, 2018, page 69.

McLaughlin, Rebecca. *Confronting Christianity: 12 Hard Questions for the Worlds Largest Religion.* Wheaton: Crossway, 2019, page 218.

PART EIGHT

Gaventa, Beverly Roberts. *First and Second Thessalonians.* Louisville, KY: Westminster John Knox Press, 2012, page 117.

Stott, John R. W. T*he Message of 1 & 2 Thessalonians.* Downers Grove, IL, U.S.A.: InterVarsity Press, 1994, page 158.

PART NINE

DeMuth, Mary E. *Pray Every Day: 90 Days of Prayer from Gods Word.* Eugene, OR: Harvest House Publishers, 2020, page 8.

Imes, Carmen Joy. *Bearing Gods Name: Why Sinai Still Matters.* Downers Grove, IL: InterVarsity Press, 2019, page 182.

READING LOG

PART	METHOD

Repetitive reading
shapes your
understanding of
the Bible.

/01
DATE:
○ 1 Thess.
○○ 1 Thess. 1:1

○ Silently to yourself
○ Out loud
○ Writing out the verses
○ Listening to the text

Continuing to
reread the text as
you progress in
your study brings
each section into
a clearer focus,
answers prolonged
questions, and sears
the scriptures into
your heart and mind.

/02
DATE:
○ 1 Thess.
○○ 1 Thess. 1:2–10

○ Silently to yourself
○ Out loud
○ Writing out the verses
○ Listening to the text

/03
DATE:
○ 1 Thess.
○○ 1 Thess. 2:1–16

○ Silently to yourself
○ Out loud
○ Writing out the verses
○ Listening to the text

/04
DATE:
○ 1 Thess.
○○ 1 Thess. 2:17–3:13

○ Silently to yourself
○ Out loud
○ Writing out the verses
○ Listening to the text

/05
DATE:
○ 1 Thess.
○○ 1 Thess. 4:1–18

○ Silently to yourself
○ Out loud
○ Writing out the verses
○ Listening to the text

/06
DATE:
○ 1 Thess.
○○ 1 Thess. 5:1–28

○ Silently to yourself
○ Out loud
○ Writing out the verses
○ Listening to the text

/07
DATE:
○ 2 Thess.
○○ 2 Thess. 1:1–12

○ Silently to yourself
○ Out loud
○ Writing out the verses
○ Listening to the text

/08
DATE:
○ 2 Thess.
○○ 2 Thess. 2:1–17

○ Silently to yourself
○ Out loud
○ Writing out the verses
○ Listening to the text

/09
DATE:
○ 2 Thess.
○○ 2 Thess. 3:1–18

○ Silently to yourself
○ Out loud
○ Writing out the verses
○ Listening to the text

INCOMMUNICABLE

THE ATTRIBUTES OF GOD

TRANSCENDENT
God's transcendence defines his otherness from creation. | There is no one like God. As creator and ruler of all things, he exists beyond our reason and outside of our categories—including space and time. He is a God of mystery who defies description.

INFINITE
God's infiniteness describes the abundance of his existence. | God is completely unbound by limits. There is no way to measure his character and no beginning or end to his existence. Because he possesses the fullness of all his attributes he depends on no person or thing to provide him life.

IMMANENT
God's immanence describes his active participation in the world. | As creator and ruler of all things his creation depends on him to provide for, protect, and sustain what he has made. As he draws near to and interacts with humanity, he reveals and brings about his divine purposes and plan.

IMMUTABLE
God's immutability describes the consistency of his character. | God cannot change. He is exactly who is— he cannot increase or decrease in any of his attributes. He does exactly what he declares he will do—his plans and promises remain sure and certain. Everything about God is dependable and trustworthy.

OMNIPOTENT
God's omnipotence describes the fullness of his power. | God possesses all power and authority. Without any effort on his part he can bring about whatever he desires.

OMNIPRESENT
God's omnipresence describes the fullness of his presence. | God is unbound by place and time. He is present everywhere, in all time—past, present, and future. Instead of being spread thin, God's presence fills the earth without sacrificing any of his attention or care.

OMNISCIENT
God's omniscience describes the fullness of his knowledge. | God has nothing to learn because he knows all things about everyone, every place, and everything. Unbound by time, his knowledge extends into eternity past and eternity future. He doesn't wonder, he doesn't discover, and he is never taken by surprise.

SOVEREIGN
God's sovereignty describes his place as ruler over all creation. | God's universal authority encompasses everyone and everything. He reigns over the world conforming everything to his own will and bringing about his divine purposes. In all of his ways he is unthwarted and unstoppable.

HOLY

God's holiness is a fusion of his purity and power. | He is utterly good and completely powerful. And God alone is able to make everything and everyone perfect as well.

JUST

God's justice is the loving action of an all-powerful God to right what is wrong. | God's justice always brings about equality, punishes rightly, and vindicates the offended.

LOVE

God's love is his loyal affection and care. God's love exists perfectly within himself and radiates out to encompass all he has created. Everything God does he does out of love.

MERCIFUL

God's mercy is his compassion on display. | Because God wants to forge a relationship with humanity despite its rebellion against him, he withholds his judgment and works in ways that ultimately benefit his people and create the provision of salvation.

PATIENCE

God's patience is his ability to wait confidently for the completion of his perfect purposes. | Because God possesses divine perspective and a desire for people to repent, he bears with humankind through every moral failure. He is longsuffering and slow to anger.

WISE

God's wisdom is his perfect insight on all things. | As creator, ruler, and all-knowing divinity, God understands everything exactly the right way and determines the perfect ends and means in all situations. He directs the path that leads to abundant life.

FAITHFUL

God's faithfulness is his commitment to keep his promises. | God is always trustworthy to act in accordance with his character and to save, sustain, and sanctify his people.

TRUTH

God's truthfulness is his expression of the world just as he created it. | As the origin of all things, God determines and declares what is right and good and what is wrong and evil. He delights in revealing how people can live in right relationship with him and with each other.

GRACE

God's graciousness is his choice to give abundant life to the undeserving. | No one deserves or can earn anything from God. Despite humanity's rejection of God, he displays his extravagant love by offering salvation through Jesus Christ and guidance in living a life pleasing to him.

COMMUNICABLE

BELONGING

TO THE DAY